Londoners
through a lens

timeout.com

Published by Time Out Guides Ltd, a wholly owned subsidiary of Time Out Group Ltd.
Time Out and the Time Out logo are trademarks of Time Out Group Ltd.

© **Time Out Group Ltd 2009**

10 9 8 7 6 5 4 3 2 1

This edition first published in Great Britain in 2009 by Ebury Publishing
A Random House Group Company
20 Vauxhall Bridge Road, London SW1V 2SA

Random House Australia Pty Limited 20 Alfred Street, Milsons Point, Sydney, New South Wales 2061, Australia
Random House New Zealand Limited 18 Poland Road, Glenfield, Auckland 10, New Zealand
Random House South Africa (Pty) Limited Isle of Houghton, Corner Boundary Road & Carse O'Gowrie,
Houghton 2198, South Africa

Random House UK Limited Reg. No. 954009

Distributed in USA by Publishers Group West
1700 Fourth Street, Berkeley, California 94710

Distributed in Canada by Publishers Group Canada
250A Carlton Street, Toronto, Ontario M5A 2L1

For further distribution details, see www.timeout.com

ISBN: 978-1-84670-161-0

A CIP catalogue record for this book is available from the British Library

Printed and bound in Singapore by Tien Wah Press Ltd

The Random House Group Limited supports The Forest Stewardship Council (FSC), the leading international
forest certification organisation. All our titles that are printed on Greenpeace approved FSC certified paper carry
the FSC logo. Our paper procurement policy can be found at www.rbooks.co.uk/environment.

Time Out carbon-offsets all its flights with Trees for Cities (www.treesforcities.org).

Time Out Guides Limited
Universal House
251 Tottenham Court Road
London W1T 7AB
Tel + 44 (0)20 7813 3000
Fax + 44 (0)20 7813 6001
Email guides@timeout.com
www.timeout.com

Editorial
Editor Cath Phillips
Proofreader Marion Moisy
Indexer Holly Pick

Managing Director Peter Fiennes
Editorial Director Sarah Guy
Series Editor Cath Phillips
Business Manager Dan Allen
Editorial Manager Holly Pick
Assistant Management Accountant
Ija Krasnikova

Design
Art Director Scott Moore
Art Editor Pinelope Kourmouzoglou
Senior Designer Henry Elphick
Graphic Designers Kei Ishimaru, Nicola Wilson
Digital Imaging Tessa Kar

Picture Desk
Picture Editor Jael Marschner
Deputy Picture Editor Lynn Chambers
Picture Researcher Gemma Walters
Picture Librarian Christina Theisen
Picture Desk Assistant Marzena Zoladz

Advertising
Commercial Director Mark Phillips
Sales Manager Alison Wallen

Marketing
Marketing Manager Yvonne Poon
Sales & Marketing Director North America Lisa Levinson
Senior Publishing Brand Manager Luthfa Begum
Art Director Anthony Huggins

Production
Group Production Director Mark Lamond
Production Manager Brendan McKeown
Production Controller Damian Bennett
Production Coordinator Kelly Fenlon

Time Out Group
Chairman Tony Elliott
Chief Executive Officer David King
Group General Manager/Director Nichola Coulthard
Time Out Communications Ltd MD David Pepper
Time Out International Ltd MD Cathy Runciman
Time Out Magazine Ltd Publisher/MD Mark Elliott
Group IT Director Simon Chappell
Marketing & Circulation Director Catherine Demajo

Contributors Fiona Barrows, Will Fulford-Jones, Jan Fuscoe, Hugh Graham, Sarah Guy, Sally Harrild, Ronnie Haydon, Anna Norman, Charlotte Thomas, Sarah Thorowgood, Yolanda Zappaterra.

The Editor would like to thank Alexia Shaw and Caroline Theakstone at Getty Images, Sarah Guy, Pete Watts.

Photography Getty Images, www.gettyimages.com.

Contents

Introduction

What links Harold Pinter, mods on their souped-up scooters, Linton Kwesi Johnson, children reading a comic, Harry Gordon Selfridge, Arsenal fans and Ruth Ellis? Not much, it seems. Well, they're all Londoners in one way or another – some were born and raised in the city, some lived and worked here, some died here – and they're all pictured in the following pages. Welcome to *Londoners through a lens*. As with its predecessor, *London through a lens*, we've plundered the vast archives of Getty Images to bring you a multifaceted selection of photographs of the capital during the past century or so (the images date from 1863 to 1997), but this time with the emphasis on its inhabitants.

London has produced its fair share of heroes and heroines (and their opposites), so you'll find plenty of well-known faces pictured here: artists and actors, musicians and murderers, playwrights and politicians, scientists and sporting stars. Some are almost defined by their London connections (step forward, Charles Dickens and Mary Quant), some discovered fame and fortune here (hats off to music hall legend Marie Lloyd and jazz club owner Ronnie Scott), while others left a legacy that stretches far beyond the city's limits (praise be to William Booth, founder of the Salvation Army).

But this isn't a celebrity identity parade; it's the anonymous Londoners, the people that haven't appeared in the spotlight (actual or metaphorical) that have shaped the metropolis of today. Without the firemen, dockers, buskers, cab drivers, flower sellers, tube workers, market stall holders, skins, punks and people just going about their everyday business, the streets of London would be dull and lifeless. So you'll find pictures of crowds and individuals doing what Londoners do best: queuing, cheering, shopping, eating, drinking, working, striking, protesting and having fun in multiple ways. Some depict places and people long gone – the dockers of the East End, for example, and, thankfully, the cat-meat sellers of Camberwell – but many emphasise the continuity of life in the capital. There will always be children running around Hyde Park and cyclists exploring the backstreets of Putney, even if bowling hoops and plus-fours are no longer essential accessories. We could, of course, have picked hundreds of other photographs, but we hope the ones we have chosen are a reminder of what makes the capital great: its people.

Cath Phillips, Editor

Memory lane

Colin Jacobson considers the complex relationship between photography, perception and the past.

Ever since the invention of the camera, photographs have been regarded as an aide-memoire, fixed references to a transitory reality that has gone before. Once taken, a photo becomes an instant historical artefact, a reminder of a moment that has disappeared forever. Thus memory and photography are inextricably linked. In a sense, memory is contained within the image itself, even if we are aware that it is our own gaze, our interaction with the picture, that sparks off a process of recollection. Little wonder that our relationship to old photos is complex – tinged with nostalgia, wonder, puzzlement and often imbued with a kind of melancholy.

It's also very easy to mock photographs of the past: the old-young faces, the weird fashions and hairstyles, the antiquated machines and equipment, the general naivety and lack of sophistication. Images of the recent past – visual reminders of our own half-forgotten biographies – can seem stranger than those from a century ago. They can even be discomforting, so that we laugh them off in a kind of voyeuristic denial.

Photography theorists have argued that images are unreliable because they can only really confirm that some person or object existed at a moment in time. What we respond to, they say, is the picture itself and not the more complex aspects – sound, smell, touch, emotion and other sensory factors – of what it felt like to be alive at the time. It's certainly true that when we look at a collection of historic photos from a city as huge and as complex as London, we bring our own personal baggage with us and read the images in myriad different ways. This reflects both the power of a photograph to stimulate imagination and its tendency to beguile us into some kind of personal appropriation of its meaning. If you're old enough to remember the Notting Hill Carnival riots of 1976 you might not recognise the particular scene depicted, but you'll certainly recall the deep sense of shock felt by many Londoners at the violence and destruction.

Looking at the past lives of Londoners through photographs, it is the social differences of then and now that strike hardest – the images of poverty, the barefoot children waiting for food during the Dock strike in 1912, the impoverished family in Shadwell in 1920. Successful photos have the power to raise awkward and sometimes unanswerable questions. This family appears to be in a state of submission in relation to the photographer, as though they did not really have much choice about having their picture taken. Was the photo ever published? What did the family feel about their image being used in this way to illustrate London's poverty? Did they want their plight to be given the oxygen of publicity? Were they coerced, persuaded, offered money or food? What happened afterwards? Did someone take up their cause?

Such ambiguity of meaning surrounds many of the photographs in this book. In the absence of the original context, the images can become symbolic or generic, resonant with a sense of old London without necessarily having a particular, identifiable story to tell. Of course, an absence of specifics can also liberate and enhance the viewer's imagination. Take the picture of anonymous evacuees at a train window in World War II – what happened to them, what kind of lives did they grow up to lead, are they still alive now? It is this kaleidoscopic rollercoaster of images on offer that makes this book both fascinating and seductive. If the past is another country, is it one we want to understand or just view as visual entertainment?

Cultural shocks abound. Is that really the Ku Klux Klan in London in 1951? Realising it was just a fancy dress parade at the Festival of Britain, and probably one depicting Catholic devotees during Holy Week rather than the KKK, does not quite diminish the sense of incredulity. Perhaps this is one of the valuable functions of visual memorabilia – to remind us how far we've come from the days of abject poverty and such insensitive social behaviour.

Inevitably, when we reflect on these pictures, we compare them with how we live now. The massive crowd watching a fire in Hackney in 1930 is intriguing because, in similar situations, we're likely to resort to TV or the internet for visual information. It's hard to imagine that the lounging Teddy boys pictured in 1955, who seem strangely benign to modern eyes, were deemed just as intimidating then as 'hoodies' are today. We may be used to hordes of football fans, but not to the use of clumsy looking megaphones for crowd control as at the Chelsea/Arsenal match in 1935.

We should expect the past to throw up visual surprises. Who would have thought to see Margaret Thatcher appearing to actually enjoy herself in a moment of frivolity in 1962? Where are the minders and bodyguards when Charlie Chaplin arrived at Paddington Station at the height of his fame in 1931? Can Humph ever have been as young and good-looking as when he was snapped with a flying dancer in 1949?

What kind of visceral response do we have to the avuncular portrait of Albert Pierrepoint, responsible for the hanging of 430 people before the abolition of capital punishment? Where are the sexual scandals to shake the nation like that of Profumo and Christine Keeler in 1963? We can marvel at the casual way famous people are depicted here and note the absence of manicured, spin-doctored image-making that we have come to expect from today's celebrities.

Most of the images in this book were taken on assignment for the many photo agencies that grew up to supply newspapers and magazines in the inter-war years. The visual story-telling is therefore mediated through the interests and demands of editors and their ideas of what their readers wanted, rather than driven by the creative choices of the photographers. Stylistically, many of the pictures are arranged, posed or set up with a simplified, easy-to-digest feel, getting the point across in a straightforward, graphically successful way. They are designed to illustrate journalistic news or feature stories, rather than to provide a profound interpretation of society – though they nevertheless offer neat slices of time when viewed retrospectively. Here and there a different kind of approach is evident; the documentary and reportage work of John Thomson, Paul Martin and many of the *Picture Post* photographers represents a more genuine attempt to observe and reflect social reality, rather than to force it into a preconceived formulaic mould.

What emerges from this collection more than anything is the relative innocence of the relationship between photographer and subject in the past, even in a knowing city like London. Nowadays, there's a growing suspicion about the motives of photographers and the uses to which their images might be put. Some commentators identify the death of Princess Diana in 1997 as the moment attitudes changed – certainly, many reputable photographers were threatened or assaulted in the aftermath of that event.

Photographers continue to take an interest in Londoners' lives, but in a more guarded, muted way. Current manners and the survival instinct require an element of permission to enter into the photographic pact, especially in the tougher parts of the capital, limiting the possibility of capturing authentically observed moments on the street. It is unlikely that such a wide-ranging and vibrant visual compilation about Londoners and their lives will ever be possible in times to come.

Colin Jacobson is Senior Lecturer in Photojournalism at the University of Westminster.

Gilbert and George 1981

The Morecambe & Wise of the art world, the double act that is Gilbert and George has long been a familiar sight around Spitalfields, where they have lived and worked since the late 1960s. The pair – Gilbert Prousch (right) and George Passmore, pictured at their Fournier Street home – met while studying sculpture at St Martins School of Art in 1967. They talk of themselves as 'living sculptures' and are as famous for their eccentric habits (trademark suits, deadpan expressions, sentences prefixed by the royal 'we', daily meal at the same Turkish restaurant in Dalston) as their work is notorious for its conflation of nudity, scatology, religion and patriotism. Regular walks around east London provide the imagery and inspiration for their work; as George has observed: 'Nothing happens in the world that doesn't happen in the East End.'

David Corio/Michael Ochs Archive

Michael Caine and Bobby Moore 1981

Michael Caine (born Maurice Micklewhite in Rotherhithe in 1933) and footballing legend Bobby Moore (born in Barnet in 1941) pose at the charity première of *Escape to Victory*. The John Huston-directed movie about a football match between Allied POWs and Germans in World War II wasn't a huge critical success, but it garnered much attention because of its high-profile cast; as well as Caine, king of British cinema since the '60s thanks to the likes of *Alfie*, *The Italian Job* and *Get Carter*, and Moore, a national hero after leading England to World Cup success in 1966, it also starred Sylvester Stallone (in the unlikely role of a goalie), Max von Sydow and footballers Pelé and Osvaldo Ardiles (plus a host of Ipswich Town players).

Ray Moreton/Keystone/Hulton Archive

Pearly children 1913

The origins of Cockney London's pearly monarchy are vague. One account points to the practice of costermongers (fruit and vegetable traders) of distinguishing themselves from other workers by decorating their trousers and waistcoats with a row of mother-of-pearl buttons; by the 18th century they were electing their own 'Coster King' to protect their interests and raise money for costers who had fallen on hard times. Another version centres on orphaned roadsweeper Henry Croft, who used pearl buttons salvaged from a Thames boatwreck in the 1880s to embellish his suit, hat and stick – and then started raising money for his orphanage. Charity work and costumes covered with 'flashies' have remained central to the role of the pearlies. Their annual Harvest Festival services – at St Paul's in Covent Garden or St Martin's-in-the-Fields in Trafalgar Square – are still worth a butcher's.

Topical Press Agency/Hulton Archive

Whitechapel 1938

An alleyway off Whitechapel High Street presents a multicultural front for a feature about the area and its people in Picture Post magazine, with pictures by photographer and artist Humphrey Spender (brother of poet Stephen). The history of the East End is bound up with immigration, and Whitechapel's large Jewish population gave the area a distinctive flavour in the 1930s, thanks to the preponderance of Hebrew newspapers and bookshops, ritual slaughterhouses and savings banks, plus a Yiddish theatre and library, and a synagogue on Brick Lane (now a mosque). There were also considerable communities of Russians and Poles, as well as West Indian and Asian seamen. Despite being one of London's poorest and most neglected districts, Whitechapel had its charms; the article's writer, East Ender-turned-novelist William Cameron, claimed: 'The meanest street in Whitechapel has a positive quality that you will find nowhere else in London.'

Humphrey Spender/Picture Post/Hulton Archive

Benjamin Britten and Eric Crozier 1945

English composer Benjamin Britten (left), with producer and long-time collaborator Eric Crozier, examine the finer points of the set for Britten's *Peter Grimes*. The opera, the first to be performed at Sadler's Wells after a five-year dark period caused by World War II, was inspired by curate-poet George Crabbe's descriptions of the lives of people on the Suffolk coast. It was a risky venture – Britten was pretty much an unknown quantity as an opera composer, and *Peter Grimes* was his first full-length opera. But the production was a huge success and helped establish London as a major centre for opera and Britten as a composer of international renown.

Alex Bender/Picture Post/Hulton Archive

Quant and Sassoon 1964

From simple white plastic collars and black stretch stockings, Blackheath-born Mary Quant progressed to become the quintessential Swinging Sixties fashion designer, credited with inventing everything from the mini skirt to hot pants and patterned tights to paintbox make-up. Her association with hairdresser Vidal Sassoon began in 1957; by the time this picture was taken, Sassoon's bob of 1963 was world-famous, and the beginnings of the geometric style that would soon become just as celebrated are evident. Sassoon grew up in Whitechapel and as a youth belonged to the tough 43 Group of Jewish servicemen who fought Oswald Mosley's blackshirts in pitched street battles across London during the late 1940s.

Ronald Dumont/Hulton Archive

Taxidermy in Eltham 1932

A bird taxidermist, aptly named Thomas Sparrow, induges his grandson by allowing him to help out at his workshop on the even more appropriately named Sparrows Lane (just outside Charlton Athletic football ground) in Eltham. Although animals had been crudely stuffed since the late 1700s, the fashion for the expert preservation of dead animals as we know it today only really took off in the early 20th century. It was an art requiring intricate anatomical knowledge as well as considerable creativity and sculpting skills, and we'd like to think it was a self-fulfilling prophecy that led Mr Sparrow into this line of work.

Fox Photos/Hulton Archive

The Byrds 1965

Californian folk rockers the Byrds (left to right: Roger McGuinn, Chris Hillman, Mike Clarke, Gene Clark, Dave Crosby) kick off an August of English gigs with a spot of pigeon feeding in Trafalgar Square. Cue a welter of headlines about Byrds and birds. The tour rode the wave of popularity following the band's jingle-jangle cover of Bob Dylan's 'Mr Tambourine Man'. A highly influential song, it was said to have inspired George Harrison and John Lennon to buy 12-string Rickenbacker guitars just like McGuinn's. The single topped the charts on both sides of the Atlantic and stands at number 79 on *Rolling Stone*'s list of 500 Greatest Songs of All Time (Dylan's version is 106).
Victor Blackman/Express/Hulton Archive

William Morris and Edward Burne-Jones
1890

In contrast to the stiff studio portraits of the day, this casual pose of Arts and Crafts guru William Morris and Pre-Raphaelite painter Edward Burne-Jones speaks volumes about their progressive attitudes. Morris – artist, designer, writer and socialist – was born in Walthamstow in 1834 and spent his childhood roaming Epping Forest. In 1859, he teamed up with Burne-Jones to design and decorate Red House, in the outer London suburb of Bexleyheath. Two years later, the pair formed the decorative arts firm of Morris, Marshall, Faulkner & Co, based in Red Lion Square, Holborn. Morris's legacy endures, from his views on the environment and keeping things local to his ubiquitous Liberty prints. Apart from the Red House (now owned by the National Trust), the William Morris Gallery in Walthamstow and Merton Abbey Mills, his tapestry factory in Colliers Wood, are also open to the public.

Hulton Archive

Barbara Windsor
1955

Eighteen-year-old emerging star Barbara Windsor (right) enjoys the thrill of the fair at Battersea Festival Gardens with Patricia Start, a fellow student at the Aida Foster Dancing School in Golders Green. Shoreditch-born Babs (née Barbara-Ann Deeks) had made her film debut the previous year as an unnamed student in *The Belles of St Trinian's*, following in the showbiz footsteps of her great-grandmother, Fat Nan, who as a teenager performed at the Britannia Theatre in Hoxton. Grandma's career was short-lived (she went on to work in the Pimms factory), but Babs went on to fame not just in the Carry On films and London soap *EastEnders*, but in a personal life that included marriage to notorious London gangster Ronnie Knight and an alleged affair with Reggie Kray.

John Pratt/Hulton Archive

Ossie and Celia 1971

This photo of fashion designer Ossie Clark and his wife, textile designer Celia Birtwell, has echoes of their friend David Hockney's celebrated painting of the duo from the same year, 'Mr and Mrs Clark and Percy' – including the white cat (not, in fact, named Percy). The couple met at college in Manchester, but found fame while living in Notting Hill, where they collaborated on collections for King's Road boutique Quorum. Clark's flamboyant designs were snapped up by the rich and famous – Mick Jagger, the Beatles, Marianne Faithfull – but his hedonistic lifestyle, along with his homosexual affairs, sounded the death knell for his marriage. Clark was stabbed to death in his west London flat in 1996 by his former Italian lover. Birtwell continues to design and recently produced a hugely popular collection for TopShop.

Evening Standard/Hulton Archive

Busby maker 1928

A hatmaker's model tries on the wicker frame of a busby hat for size. Originally a military head-dress worn by 19th-century Hungarian hussars, the fur busby was especially popular with certain sections of the British cavalry in the years leading up to World War I. By the 1920s, however, it was increasingly outmoded and used mainly for ceremonial purposes. Nowadays it is worn by the King's Troop of the Royal Horse Artillery, who take part in the Trooping of the Colour to celebrate the Queen's official birthday, alongside the Foot Guards, who wear the taller bearskin. Both items of headgear have become the focus of attention as animal-rights campaigners question the need for the continuing use of real fur.

Fox Photos/Hulton Archive

Brixton riots 1981

13 April 1981: local residents dazedly walk past the burnt-out Windsor Castle pub on Maynall Road in Brixton after a second night of rioting in the area. Following years of escalating racial tension, heightened by mass unemployment, high crime rates and heavy-handed policing – particularly the deeply unpopular 'sus' law that allowed police to arbitrarily stop and search people for suspicious behaviour – race riots took place in Tottenham, Peckham and twice in Brixton. Scores of cars and buildings were torched, shops were looted and nearly 300 police officers and more than 60 members of the public were injured. In the public enquiry into the riots, Lord Scarman was heavily critical of the Metropolitan Police, and the sus laws were dropped.

Keystone/Hulton Archive

Charlie Chaplin 1931

Charlie Chaplin was a huge star when he arrived at Paddington Station in February 1931, classic comedies such as *The Gold Rush* (1925) and *The Circus* (1928) having endeared him to a massive worldwide audience, and made him the first actor to appear on the cover of *Time* magazine. It was an achievement that was all the more remarkable given his troubled and poverty-stricken upbringing. Born in Walworth in 1889 to music hall parents, his formative years were spent in a workhouse and home for paupers after his father died of alcoholism when Chaplin was 12, and his mother spent many years in a mental asylum – experiences that informed his work and lent his comedy a universal pathos that lasted throughout his life.

Topical Press Agency/Hulton Archive

Meryvn Peake 1946

Mervyn Peake reclines on his sofa in a shoot for *Picture Post* magazine the year that *Titus Groan*, the first book in his Gormenghast series was published. Born in China, where his parents were missionaries, Peak spent his early childhood there before moving to Wallington, Surrey, on the outskirts of London, and then studying at Croydon School of Art and the Royal Academy. He first hit his peak as an artist and illustrator (including a stint as a war artist, when he was one of the first civilians to visit Bergen-Belsen concentration camp). *Gormenghast* followed in 1950 and *Titus Alone* in 1959; more books were planned, but ill-health and an early death, at the age of 57, meant the work – now a classic of fantastical literature – remained a trilogy.

Raymond Kleboe/Picture Post/Hulton Archive

Elton John 1972

A 25-year-old Elton John displays early exhibitionist tendencies in this 1972 Terry O'Neill shot of him at the piano. From the age of 11 the gifted Reginald Kenneth Dwight had been travelling into central London from his home in Pinner to take piano lessons at the Royal Academy of Music, to which he'd won a scholarship – though it's unlikely he learned such exuberant playing there. That probably came from his love of 1950s rock 'n' roll, picked up from his parents' collection of Bill Haley, Jerry Lee Lewis and Elvis Presley records. Elton was already famous by the time this photo was taken, thanks to his songwriting partnership with Bernie Taupin, but mega-stardom was just around the corner: the album *Honky Château*, released the same year, made number one in the US charts, with the single 'Rocket Man' launching a string of Top 20 hits.

Terry O'Neill

Fascist rally at Earl's Court 1939

This British Union of Fascists meeting at Earl's Court, just two months before the outbreak of World War II, saw Oswald Mosley make a two-hour speech to a crowd of between 10,000 (*Daily Mirror*) and nearly 30,000 (*The Times*). Trotskyists and anti-fascist militants demonstrated outside; the Young Communist League of London was absent, having taken the day off for a countryside ramble. *Picture Post*'s report mocked the event, saying Mosley's gesticulations resembled someone trying 'to score a double-twenty on the dart board' while his oratorical style was reminiscent of 'a car speeding up to the next gear-change'. A year later, the BUF was banned outright and Mosley, with his wife Diana Mitford and 740 other fascists, were interned until 1943.

Humphrey Spender/Picture Post/Hulton Archive

Graham Greene 1949

Catholic convert and celebrated novelist Graham Greene is captured in a slyly knowing portrait at his London home in 1949. Eleven years after the huge critical and popular success of *Brighton Rock* (the first of the four religious novels in which the author wrestled with troublesome theological issues), Greene had become a bon viveur, raconteur and radical, who stood out for a number of daring attitudes and actions. In his lifetime he was charged with sadism, anti-Semitism, alcoholism, homosexuality and even implication in a gruesome murder, he visited brothels, was a persistent adulterer and a lifelong friend to the KGB agent Kim Philby... not to mention late nights in Havana with Fidel Castro and a fortune told by Truman Capote.

Popperfoto

Abram Games 1940

Poster boy for the golden age of graphic design, Abram Games presents his 'Blonde Bombshell' advertisement for the Auxiliary Territorial Service. Famous though the image became, at the time it was criticised by Winston Churchill, who believed it misled young women into believing that the workaday ATS was glamorous. The poster was one of more than 100 that Games created for the war effort. Born Abraham Gamse in Whitechapel, he was a pupil at Hackney Downs Grammar School (where Harold Pinter and Stephen Berkoff later studied) before heading to St Martin's School of Art – for just two terms. Games worked mainly from home in Golders Green, creating classic posters for the likes of Guinness and the Royal Shakespeare Company as well as the logo for the Festival of Britain. Layers of meaning were worked into the clean, spare lines of his designs: 'Maximum meaning, minimum means' was his motto.

Hulton Archive

Serpentine 'iceman' 1930

Ever since its founding in 1774, the Royal Humane Society has been responsible for safeguarding Londoners frolicking in the Serpentine in Hyde Park, its members (many of them volunteers) rescuing and resuscitating those in trouble. The lake is still a popular swimming spot, but skating was once a common activity too, as the water frequently froze; in 1814 a winter fair was even held on the ice. Here, an 'iceman' – wearing a belt of cork floats for his own safety – heads off the danger with a sign and the threat of a fine for anyone tempted on to the thawing lake. The RHS also gives out awards to people who have saved lives. Notable recipients include Isambard Kingdom Brunel for rescuing five men during the building of the Thames Tunnel, and Bram Stoker, for attempting to save a man from drowning in the Thames.

Keystone/Hulton Archive

Beating the bounds 1910

Edwardian youngsters prepare for one of the stranger ceremonies to still exist in London. 'Beating the bounds' – in which children who live within the 'liberty' of the Tower of London hit the markers defining the fortress's boundaries with long willow wands – still takes place, albeit only once every three years, with Beefeaters leading a procession around the Tower. Similar customs existed in ancient Greece and Rome, and evidence suggests it first appeared in Britain in pagan times (the willow being significant as a sacred tree of the Druids) before being appropriated as a Christian ritual, held on Ascension Day, to mark out parish boundaries. Fortunately for these youngsters, the practice of holding boys upside-down and bumping their heads on stone boundary markers was not part of this particular version, as it was in some rural parishes.

Hulton Archive

Robert Baden-Powell 1928

Robert Baden-Powell is surrounded by cheering Scouts at a rally in East Ham, 20 years after the publication of his book *Scouting for Boys*. B-P was already a national hero in 1908, thanks to his command of the British garrison during the Siege (and then Relief) of Mafeking in the Second Boer War, but his 'handbook for instruction in good citizenship' made him a figure of international renown. An instant bestseller, this idiosyncratic mix of personal anecdote, adventure stories, bushcraft lore and moral homilies spawned the Boy Scout (and later Girl Guide) movement, now a worldwide phenomenon with 38 million members in 216 countries. A blue plaque marks the Chief Scout's home at 9 Hyde Park Gate, SW7, and St James's Church in Paddington, where he was baptised, contains a stained-glass memorial window.

Fox Photos/Hulton Archive

Old Bob the busman 1932

Bob Smith was an unusual kind of horse trainer. By the time this portrait was taken, the 73-year-old had spent the best part of his life driving horse buses for Tillings of Peckham (the first bus company to stop at predetermined points and to operate to a fixed timetable), but had retired from driving to look after the firm's sick horses and train young ones for work on the capital's streets. Horse buses, which had been transporting Londoners since George Shillibeer launched his 'omnibus' service in 1829, were no longer in use by the 1930s – they had been largely replaced by motor buses before the Great War (when the remaining animals were requisitioned by the army), but Tillings still kept a small number of horses for hire to other firms for hauling goods vehicles, cabs and carriages.

Fox Photos/Hulton Archive

David Attenborough 1965

A confident-looking David Attenborough takes on the job of controller of BBC2 with plenty of ideas up his sleeve. Born in London and a graduate in natural sciences, he'd originally joined the Corporation on a traineeship programme and had combined the two callings with a series of globetrotting broadcasts for the series *Zoo Quest* in the 1950s. BBC2 was only a year old when he took over – 'so I could suggest anything'. He stayed until 1969, overseeing the introduction of colour television to Britain, before going on to write and present a non-stop array of landmark natural history programmes and in the process become the nation's favourite and most trusted broadcaster.

David Cairns/Hulton Archive

Grocer's shop in Nunhead 1900

A grocer on Evelina Road, Nunhead's high street, lays out his stock on the street. Everyday staples include much the same items as today: Bovril, tea, cheese, bacon, butter and margarine. It was about this time that Nunhead became part of the metropolitan borough of Camberwell, having slowly developed into a smart Victorian suburb. Vestiges of the era live on in the 19th-century terraces still standing among the local authority estates that proliferated in the 20th century. The area is probably best known for its huge Victorian cemetery, built in 1840 and one of the capital's 'Magnificent Seven' graveyards, another sign of the area's population growth during this period.

Keystone/Hulton Archive

Jack Hobbs 1925

Jack Hobbs made his cricketing debut in 1905 against the Gentlemen of England; WG Grace, the Gentlemen's captain, commented 'He's going to be a good 'un', and so he was, collecting 61,237 runs and 197 centuries in his career. Nicknamed 'the Master', he was the first English cricketer to be knighted; the main entrance to the Oval is still called the Hobbs Gate, and the Master's Club there has an annual lunch in his honour: tomato soup, roast lamb and apple pie (his favourite). Hobbs lived for many years at 17 Englewood Road in Clapham (there's a blue plaque outside) and his sports goods shop was a Fleet Street fixture for five decades. Hobbs regularly served behind the counter, and maintained he made more money there than playing cricket.

Central Press/Hulton Archive

Annie Besant
1895

Clapham-born Annie Besant (née Wood) was a social reformer and fearlessly progressive thinker. At various times a member of the Fabian Society, the National Secular Society, the Theosophical Society and also a Marxist, she was an inspiring writer, lecturer and campaigner. She was (unsuccessfully) prosecuted for co-publishing, with fellow atheist and radical Charles Bradlaugh, Charles Knowlton's book *The Fruits of Philosophy*, which promoted the use of birth control. Her campaign to improve working conditions for girls in the Bryant & May match factory in Bow earned her a blue plaque on the site in Fairfield Road, E3. Latterly, she became involved in the Indian nationalist movement, and died in India in 1933.

London Stereoscopic Company/Hulton Archive

Fake stockings 1941

The introduction of clothing rationing in 1941 caused all sorts of problems for the fashion-conscious woman, not least the resulting shortage of stockings. Silk and nylon were needed to make parachutes and barrage balloons, so many women resorted to staining their legs – with weak tea, watered-down gravy or a mix of sand and water – to give the impression that they were wearing stockings; seams were added with an eyebrow pencil. Here a customer gets the professional touch at the newly opened Bare Leg Beauty Bar at Kennards department store in Croydon. Kennards, 'the Wonder Store of the South', was a much-loved local landmark from the 1940s until its closure in 1973, famed for its in-house promotions and glitzy arcade with its mini zoo, pony rides and mock Tudor design.
Keystone/Hulton Archive

Mods in Peckham 1964

The mod subculture in Britain hit its peak in the early 1960s. Centred on a lifestyle that twinned sharp tailoring with a musical taste taking in Jamaican ska, American soul and British R&B, mods are now most closely associated with their predilection for Italian scooters and the near-obligatory military parkas that accompanied them. Vespas and Lambrettas, the scooters of choice, would be modified by the addition of mirrors and headlamps and custom chrome and paint jobs. It was London mods clashing with rockers in Clacton in 1964 that sparked the infamous seaside battles of the '60s, but there was plenty of territorial infighting too, with south London mods such as these, outside the Peckham Labour Exchange, often engaging with rival north London gangs.
Popperfoto

Cycling in Putney 1890

The song 'Daisy Bell', with its refrain 'But you'll look sweet upon the seat/Of a bicycle built for two', was a hit in London music halls in the 1890s – aptly enough if this tandem penny farthing tricycle was typical of the times. It certainly looks a lot easier (and safer) to ride than the single-person version, the 'high' or 'ordinary', although that was already obsolete by the time this picture was taken, thanks to the invention of the chain-driven, diamond-framed Rover safety bicycle. First mentioned in the Domesday Book, Putney was a fashionable suburb by the 1700s, but remained essentially rural, strung with fields and market gardens, despite the arrival of the railway in 1846. Development mushroomed in the late Victorian and Edwardian periods, but the area was not fully built up until the eve of World War I.

Sean Sexton/Hulton Archive

Amy Johnson 1930

Amy Johnson swings her legs atop her De Havilland Gipsy Moth at Hendon's Stag Lane airfield in March 1930, just five weeks before her record-breaking flight from England to Australia. She was hardly an experienced aviator at this point, having enrolled for flying lessons just 18 months before her epic flight, gaining her pilot's licence in 1929. She took 19 days to become the first solo woman to complete the 11,000-mile flight, and became an instant celebrity: adoring crowds lined the route from Croydon airport to the West End to welcome her home. The plane is now on display in the Science Museum. Her death in 1941 – ditching into the Thames Estuary while delivering a plane for the Air Transport Auxiliary – sparked rumours about spying missions, and remains something of a mystery.

Popperfoto

Model plane fans in Wimbledon 1930

Model aeroplane enthusiasts take advantage of a fair June day in 1930 to fly their machines on Wimbledon Common. Following World War I, aviation technology came on apace and the changes in model aircraft soon mirrored them. The dazzling excitement of flying gripped the world and since few had the opportunity to experience the real thing, model planes became hugely popular. Wimbledon Common was the location for many model flying competitions and drew competitors from all over the world to pit their own home-made creations against the best of British amateur aeronautical expertise.

Fox Photos/Hulton Archive

Fire in Hackney 1930

Londoners love a good spectacle, and the sight of firemen battling a major blaze at Messrs Polikoff in Mare Street was obviously dramatic enough to draw this huge crowd, held back by only a line of policeman and a solitary police horse. Alfred Polikoff's clothing factory (built in 1915 and located at the bottom of the Narrow Way) was destroyed by another fire a couple of years later. The firm moved to new premises in nearby Chatham Place and continued as a major player in Hackney's rag trade into the 1970s – still under the Polikoff name although the company had been acquired by Great Universal Stores in 1948. Burberry (also part of GUS) moved in during the 1950s, and the building is now the Burberry factory outlet, one of east London's must-visit attractions for cash-strapped fashionistas.

Fox Photos/Hulton Archive

The Beatles 1969

On 30 January 1969 the Beatles performed their last ever public concert, on the roof of the Apple building in Savile Row for Michael Lindsey-Hogg's documentary *Let It Be*. It was the band's first live performance since they had stopped touring in 1965 and they managed to play five songs – including 'Don't Let Me Down', 'I've Got a Feeling' and 'Get Back' – before London bobby Ken Wharfe, the policeman sent to stop the noise, got past road manager Mal Evans's efforts to stall him. The Beatles might have taken to London's rooftops first, but others have followed in their footsteps, including Razorlight offering a celebratory set atop the Hawley Arms to mark the reopening of the famous Camden music pub in November 2008, and U2 in a surprise appearance on the roof of BBC Broadcasting House in February 2009.

Express/Hulton Archive

Laura Knight 1929

After moving to London after World War I, Laura Knight, already well established as an artist, became fascinated by the glamour and excitement of the capital's theatre, ballet and circus scenes. Her work evolved noticeably as a result; capturing the fast-paced performing arts world – here she's sketching chorus girls backstage at a circus at the Olympia Theatre – required a matching speed and accuracy of style. While her paintings of ballet dancers and clowns are sometimes dismissed as tame and populist, her position within the establishment was assured: in 1929 she was the first female artist to be made a Dame, and in 1936 she was only the second woman to be admitted to the Royal Academy.

Fox Photos/Hulton Archive

Cleaning fog lamps 1936

London's notorious fogs – first referred to as 'pea soup' in 1871 by the *New York Times* and 'smog' (a combination of fog and the smoke from soft sea-coal) by an anonymous Londoner in 1905 – often made the city's streets treacherous, especially in winter. By the 20th century the acetylene flare fog lamps being cleaned here helped visibility to some degree. Despite the chaos, crime and health problems the fogs caused, it would take the deaths of more than 4,000 people in the Great Smog (or Big Smoke) of December 1952 to see a concerted effort to rid the capital of its lethal fogs with the passing of the Clean Air Act in 1956.

Harry Todd/Fox Photos/Hulton Archive

The Who 1966

The Who had found international fame a few months before this performance in front of Tower Bridge for US TV show *Where the Action Is*, following the release of their debut album *My Generation* in 1965. The band (left to right: John Entwistle, Roger Daltrey, Keith Moon and Pete Townshend – all Londoners by birth) garnered a reputation for vigorous and sometimes aggressive performances, and were a big influence on mod culture in the 1960s and the rise of punk in the '70s, as well as more recent Britpop bands. Moon died in 1978 and Entwistle in 2002, but Townshend and Daltrey continue to perform as the Who. *Where the Action Is*, a daily rock 'n' roll show presented by Dick Clark, aired in the States from 1965 to 1967.

Micheal Ochs Archives

Burton and Taylor 1968

There was little sign of the storms that would eventually destroy the marriage of Hampstead-born Liz Taylor and her fifth husband Richard Burton as they sailed into London in February 1968 on the yacht he'd bought her the year before. The 18-berth restored Edwardian motor yacht – dubbed *Kalizma* after Burton's children Kate, Liza and Maria – offered a welcome refuge from the press and adoring crowds obsessed with the couple. When not on the yacht, Burton and Taylor's favourite London home (and honeymoon venue) was the Oliver Messel roof garden suite at the Dorchester hotel, also a favourite of Noël Coward and Marlene Dietrich.

Bob Aylott/Keystone/Hulton Archive

Wartime gardens 1942

Gardens and allotments were cultivated wherever land was spare during World War II. In London, parks, squares, school grounds, bomb craters and ruins – as seen here on the edge of the City (St Paul's Cathedral is clearly visible in the background) – were all turned into fruitful plots, and by 1943 almost half the capital's families were using allotments to top up their rations. Hyde Park had its own piggery, Kensington Gardens replaced its flowers with rows of cabbages, and St James's Square was planted with vegetables as part of the 'Dig for Victory' campaign. There were other ways to aid the war effort: air-raid shelters were built in Soho and Manchester Squares, Belgrave Square became a tank park, and Hereford Square was used as a baseball pitch by American GIs.

Hans Wild/Time Life Pictures

David Lean
1947

David Lean has a head-scratching moment while shooting his second Dickens' adaptation, *Oliver Twist*, following the success of *Great Expectations* a year earlier (both starring his long-time collaborator Alec Guinness). Autocratic, perfectionist and multi-talented, Lean worked as an editor, producer, actor and screenwriter, but it was as a director that he won global acclaim, notably with such full-blown blockbusters as *Lawrence of Arabia*, *Dr Zhivago* and *The Bridge on the River Kwai* (its theme tune, 'Colonel Bogey', was played at his memorial service at St Paul's in 1991). But many prefer his more modest early black and white films, such as *Brief Encounter*, which best capture his atmospheric, romantic, quintessentially English style of filmmaking. Born in Croydon, he lived for many years on Narrow Street in Limehouse.

Nat Farbman/Time Life Pictures

Rotten Row 1930

A couple of nannies take the air along Rotten Row in Hyde Park with their charges safely tucked up in the sturdy, no-nonsense prams typical of the day. The sand-covered avenue running from Hyde Park Corner along the south side of the park was established by William III after the court moved to Kensington Palace at the end of the 17th century; it was lit with 300 oil lamps from as early as 1690, making it the first artificially lit highway in Britain. Rotten Row's heyday was the 18th and 19th centuries, when it was the place to see and be seen as the city's gentry paraded up and down of a summer's evening. Although considerably less busy with horse traffic these days, it's still maintained as a bridleway and popular with members of the Household Cavalry, whose stables are nearby.

Fox Photos/Hulton Archive

Michael Powell 1947

English director Michael Powell and Hungarian writer Emeric Pressburger were the dynamic duo of 1940s British filmmaking behind such masterpieces as *The Life and Death of Colonel Blimp* and *A Matter of Life and Death*. Crowds gathered as *The Red Shoes* – their 1948 Technicolor classic inspired by Hans Christian Andersen's tale of magic crimson slippers – was filmed in Covent Garden (Powell is on the left of the camera). Scenes were also shot inside the Royal Opera House and Notting Hill's Mercury Theatre, where Moira Shearer's character, Vicky, dances *Swan Lake*. Shearer was a ballerina at Sadler's Wells at the time and had no acting experience; her first foray into the movies turned her into a huge star.
Keystone/Hulton Archive

The Islington twins 1981

From the early 1980s into the '90s, identical twins Chet and Joe Okonkwo (aka Chuka and Dubem, or the Islington twins) were a regular sight around Highbury & Islington Station, where the eccentric duo enthralled hangers-on with their idiosyncratic fashion sense and tall tales of Oxbridge country gent alter egos Charles and Roger. The sons of Nigerian Chuma Okonkwo, a broadcaster and colleague of Chinua Achebe, the identically dressed twins typifed the highly individualistic trends of the time – whether wearing tonic suits, Sta-Prest trousers, orange boilersuits or nightshirts, topped and tailed with tweed caps or straw boaters and Frank Wright loafers or Chinese slippers. They were photographed for style mags *The Face* (as here) and *i-D*. Now in their mid forties, the twins still live in London, still love a good party and still look as sharp as new pins.
Janette Beckman/Hulton Archive

Twiggy 1968

Neasden-born Lesley Hornby started modelling, under her childhood nickname, at the age of 16. As a skinny, gangling, fashion-conscious teenager, she both fed into and drove the androgynous, youth-focused aesthetic of the era, her waif-like figure and boyish short hair a distinct change from the previous decade's cinched waists, full skirts and ample busts. Twiggy rapidly became the world's first supermodel, her large eyes and fake eyelashes recognised internationally, but her career was surprisingly short-lived: she left the industry after just four years to work as an actress (most famously in Ken Russell's film *The Boy Friend*) and singer. She returned to modelling in her fifties, appearing in ad campaigns for Marks & Spencer.

Popperfoto

Pete, Dud and David 1973

Comedy duo Peter Cook and Dudley Moore entertain David Bowie backstage at the Cambridge Theatre in the West End, following their show *Behind The Fridge*. Three days later, on 12 May, Bowie would open the UK leg of his Ziggy Stardust world tour at Earl's Court. None of them was having a particularly good week. Pete and Dud's obscene songs and dark, scatological sketches – among them a conversation between a seemingly homicidal taxi driver and his panic-stricken passenger, and Moore's one-legged audition for the screen role of Tarzan – were receiving poor reviews and a muted reception. Bowie's gig was the first time the massive Earl's Court Arena had been used as a concert venue, and it was a disaster; 18,000 fans, some of them naked, drunk and pissing in the aisles, were subjected to bad sound and equally bad visibility, and a near riot stopped the show for ten minutes.

Keystone/Hulton Archive

Cinema queue 1937

Expectant school kids form an orderly queue outside the country's only children's cinema, in Plaistow Road, West Ham. They're waiting to see a matinée double-bill of *Tarzan the Fearless* and *Flash Gordon*, both starring Buster Crabbe, ex-Olympic swimmer turned Hollywood he-man. Many of the capital's music halls had transformed themselves into cinemas in the 1920s, but the '30s brought a new wave of massive, purpose-built picture houses – the biggest in east London was the Commercial Road Troxy, with 3,250 seats, though even it was dwarfed by the 4,000-seater State Kilburn, the largest cinema in England. This was a golden age of film-going; it was estimated that a third of the UK saw RKO's 1937 smash hit *Snow White and the Seven Dwarfs*.

Reg Speller/Hulton Archive

Graham Hill 1965

Formula One legend Graham Hill gets a few pointers from the boys on the Scalextric track at Springfield Youth Club in Hackney. The motor racing community helped set up the club – still going strong – and Hampstead-born Hill was its first president. By 1965, he'd already won the F1 world championship; he went on to do it again in 1968, and was also the only driver to win the Triple Crown of Motorsport. Also a keen rower, Hill was a long-standing member of the London Rowing Club, and used its insignia (eight vertical stripes representing oars) for his racing helmet. He died trying to land his light aircraft in fog in 1975, on the edge of a golf course in north London, just weeks after retiring from professional racing.
Philip Townsend/Express/Hulton Archive

Terry-Thomas 1958

Actor Terry-Thomas smiles winningly as he motors to court to face a drink-driving charge. His relatively humble beginnings – he was born the fourth of five children to a Smithfield provisions merchant in North Finchley – meant that Thomas Terry Hoar-Stevens had to work hard at his dandyish persona. A gifted mimic, he lost his north London twang and perfected the class-clown role at public school, which helped him through his lean early stage career. At the outset of World War II he signed up to the Entertainment National Service Association (ENSA); BBC work after the war gained him further recognition and his carefully assembled look – Savile Row suit, jewelled cigarette holder and devilish grin – earned him plum bounder roles at home and in Hollywood.

Popperfoto

Teddy boys in Bermondsey 1955

Hanging out on a grubby street corner in Bermondsey, three youths sport their newly aquired Teddy boy threads. Originally a fashion inspired by a conservative and Savile Row-influenced desire to once again dress men in the graceful suits of the Edwardian period, it seems only fitting that the first post-war teenagers should have hijacked the trend and made it their own. Although undeniably the badge of the first recognisably 'teenage' subculture, the often tailor-made suits, drainpipe trousers, brothel creepers and greasy 'duck's arse' hair-dos were also symptomatic of a new prosperity following the end of the war and rationing. The Picture House on the Old Kent Road (advertised in the background poster) was demolished a year after this photo was taken to make way for the Bricklayers' Arms flyover.

Popperfoto

Ernest Shackleton
1932

This statue of Sir Ernest Shackleton, on its way to the Royal Geographical Society in Kensington (where it still stands), captures the polar explorer in his element, dressed head to toe in bulky winter garments. Born in Ireland, Shackleton moved to Sydenham at the age of ten and was educated at Dulwich College, but left at 16 to go to sea. He's best remembered for the *Endurance* expedition of 1914-16; when his ship got stuck in ice and broke apart, Shackleton rowed 800 miles across the Antarctic Ocean in a lifeboat. At South Georgia, he had to scale a mountain to summon help for his crew, who were stranded on Elephant Island; all were rescued. On another voyage six years later, he died of a heart attack on South Georgia – where he is buried. Long overshadowed by Captain Scott, he's now seen as one of Britain's great explorers and true heroes.

Fox Photos/Hulton Archive

Flooding on the Lea Bridge Road 1928

Prior to the opening of the Thames Barrier in 1984, the Thames Valley suffered some severe floods, most famously in January 1928 (when this picture was taken) and in 1953, when 53 fatalities on Canvey Island led to the decision to construct the barrier. In both instances the Thames and the River Lea burst their banks – here forcing locals to queue for lorries to carry them across the submerged Lea Bridge Road. Despite the 1928 flood being less heavy than the 1953 one, the fact that it reached central London meant that death and devastation in the capital were greater; 14 people died, many drowning in basement rooms, when part of the Chelsea Embankment collapsed, some 4,000 people lost their homes and there was extensive damage to the Tate Gallery's collection.

Fox Photos/Hulton Archive

Grunwick strike 1977

In a fractious decade of labour disputes, the 1976-78 strike at the Grunwick photo-processing laboratory in Willesden was a particularly significant one; the violent clashes between pickets and police would determine the handling and direction of future conflicts – notably the miners' strike of 1983-84. In August 1976, a third of Grunwick's workers were sacked over trade union recognition. The postal workers who came out in support by refusing to deliver mail to the plant were taken to court by Grunwick's managing director George Ward, who was backed by right-wing pressure group the Freedom Association. The strike lasted two years, with Ward the eventual winner – though the affair did highlight the shocking working conditions, treatment and pay of the firm's predominately East African and South Asian female workforce.

M Fresco/Evening Standard/Hulton Archive

Jean Cocteau 1959

French poet, filmmaker, novelist and artist Jean Cocteau greatly influenced the avant-garde Surrealist group and counted among his circle Marcel Proust, Edith Piaf and Jean Marais, his lover and star of his most famous film, *La belle et la bête*. In November 1959 he spent a week in London drawing murals for Soho's Notre Dame de France church as part of the reconstruction of the building, which had been destroyed by wartime bombardment. The murals are still there; they depict the Annunciation and the Crucifixion – the latter, somewhat controversially, shows only the lower legs of the crucified Christ (partially visible to the right of the photo), and includes a self-portrait of Cocteau with his back turned to the cross.

Ron Case/Hulton Archive

Moon tourist
1956

Although it wasn't until the end of the
following decade that Neil Armstrong made
his historic landing on the moon, the 1950s
was the era when the idea of space travel
moved from the realm of science-fiction
fantasy into that of reality. Here, a space-
suited employee of a London travel agency
adds a customer to the reservation list for
a journey to the moon; the flight is scheduled
for the year 2040. A year after this photo
was taken, the USSR sent its first satellite,
Sputnik 1, into orbit. Fuelled by the Cold War,
the race to get the first man on the moon
was on between the world's superpowers,
and interest in space became widespread,
reaching all corners of popular culture.
Derek Berwin/Fox Photos/Hulton Archive

Jeremy Thorpe 1979

It's hard to imagine this dour-looking establishment gent as a famed wit and sharp political impressionist, but Jeremy Thorpe, Liberal Party leader from 1967 to 1976, had been well known as both, and for a dandyish fashion sense too. By the time this photo was taken, outside the Old Bailey on 18 June, such triviality was behind him. Thorpe had been charged with conspiracy and incitement to murder in a case dubbed 'Rinkagate', centring as it did on the death in 1975 of a great dane called Rinka and the attempted murder of a gay ex-model, Norman Scott, who claimed to have been sexually involved with Thorpe in the early '60s. The case, for which Thorpe was acquitted, had it all; shady characters, explicit personal letters, political conspiracy… unsurprisingly, it became known as 'the trial of the century'. Outside the court, gay rights supporters protested over the treatment of homosexuality during the trial.

Aubrey Hart/Hulton Archive

Christmas postman 1925

Postal deliveries have come a long way since the early 17th century, when the only things carried were letters to and from the King and the Royal Court. In 1635 King Charles I issued a proclamation extending the use of the Royal Mail to the public, and the service was enthusiastically taken up by businesses and the wealthy, who would pay for the receipt of letters, until 1680 when William Dockwra pioneered a London-wide penny post service from his office in Lime Street. This pre-payment of letters developed into an impressive system that in the capital alone saw between six and 12 daily deliveries, and grew to carry much more than letters – as this Christmas delivery of a brace of pheasants to a Chelsea address shows.

Topical Press Agency/Hulton Archive

Henry Moore
1978

An artist whose creations have had a lasting impact on London's public spaces takes a look at 'Three Way Piece: Points', which he sculpted in 1967, as it is placed at the Admiralty Arch end of the Mall following repairs. Moore claimed that 'sculpture is an art of the open air', an attitude that attracted both acclaim and controversy – when Roland Penrose exhibited Moore's 'Mother and Child' in his Hampstead garden, disgruntled neighbours initiated a press campaign against the piece. Moore spent many years in London before World War II, teaching at the Royal College of Art and Chelsea School of Art, and living in Hampstead; his wartime drawings of Londoners sleeping in the Underground won him international fame and had a lasting impact on his sculptural work.

Maurice Hibberd/Evening Standard/Hulton Archive

Regent Street hats
1967

The London Tourist Board and the Millinery Institute of Great Britain were responsible for this display of outlandish headwear on Regent Street in 1967, when they presented a 'Hatter's Tea Party' – presumably a campaign to promote the capital's fashion talent; the fur industry seems to have been involved too. From left to right, the creations are called Charmer, Butterfly, Mascarade (though this particular hat looks remarkably like the Post Office Tower, which had opened to the public the previous year) and Ice Maiden. Coincidentally, 1967 was the year that Philip Treacy, Britain's most famous hat designer of recent times, was born.
Evening Standard/Hulton Archive

Tariq Ali 1968

Tariq Ali's left-wing credentials were already cemented when this photo was taken of him, aged 24, protesting outside the Russian Embassy on 21 August, the day that the Soviet Union invaded Czechoslovakia to halt Dubcek's 'Prague Spring' liberalisation reforms. Pakistan-born Ali came to Britain to study at Oxford University in the early 1960s, soon becoming one of London's best-known members of the New Left and an outspoken critic of American foreign policy (a public profile that is still strong today; he was a core opponent of the 2003 invasion of Iraq). He may look more like a dandy than a revolutionary socialist, but 1968 was also when he joined the Trotskyist party the International Marxist Group, and took on the editorship of the newly launched radical newspaper *Black Dwarf*.

Ballard/Hulton Archive

Chelsea v Arsenal 1935

Such was the size of the crowd that came to see Arsenal take on Chelsea at Stamford Bridge on 12 October 1935 that marshalls resorted to megaphones to keep fans in order. In fact, the game's attendance of 82,905 fans has never been bettered at the ground. Arsenal won 5-2 – not surprisingly, as the 1930s was the Gunners' heyday when they won five league championships and two FA Cups – while the Blues' first major trophy didn't arrive until 1955. So dismal was their early form that vaudeville performer Norman Long recorded a comic song in 1933 called 'On the day that Chelsea went and won the Cup', which listed a series of equally improbable and strange events, such as 'The sun came out in Manchester and funny things like that… And a pigeon hatched a guinea pig and blamed it on the cat.'
Popperfoto

Quentin Crisp 1948

One of the many strange facts about gay icon, raconteur and writer Quentin Crisp (born Denis Charles Pratt in Sutton, Surrey in 1908), is that he never did any housework, believing that after four years the dirt didn't get any worse. 'It is', he advised in his 1968 autobiography *The Naked Civil Servant*, 'just a question of keeping your nerve.' Crisp developed and practised this unorthodox theory here, a scruffy bedsit at 129 Beaufort Street, Chelsea, which he occupied from 1940 until his move to New York in 1981. Paying six shillings a week to his landlady Miss Vereker, Crisp refused to decorate the flat in any way; Harold Pinter later claimed it was the inspiration for his play *The Room*. When Crisp finally quit the flat, the neighbours cheered from their windows.
Popperfoto

Peter Rachman 1960

The de facto colour bar that denied lodgings to many West Indian immigrants to London was a golden opportunity for slum landlord Peter Rachman – pictured here at his desk in central London. He bought up run-down buildings in Notting Hill, Paddington, Bayswater and North Kensington, drove out the sitting tenants and then charged the newcomers extortionate rents for squalid and overcrowded rooms; at the height of his operations, he owned about 100 mansion blocks in west London. His activities were so notorious that 'Rachmanism' has become synonymous with despicable housing practices. His extravagant and scandalous lifestyle (both Mandy Rice-Davies and Christine Keeler were his mistresses) was short-lived, however; he died, in mysterious circumstances, in 1962 at the age of 41.

Paul Popper/Popperfoto

Lunch at Lord's 1895

Well-dressed, well-heeled spectators stretch their legs at Lord's during the lunch interval of the annual summer cricket match between Eton and Harrow public schools. The match was first played in 1805 and the tradition continues today: it's the oldest fixture to be held at the ground. Lord's has long been associated with the elite, ever since the aristocrats who used to play at White Conduit Fields in Islington decided they needed their own private cricket ground to get away from the hoi polloi that gathered to watch them. In 1787 Thomas Lord, a bowler with the team, leased land on Dorset Fields in Marylebone (now Dorset Square) and thus Marylebone Cricket Club was formed. In 1814 the MCC moved to its present home in then-rural St John's Wood.

Symons & Thiele/Hulton Archive

Clapton Greyhound Stadium 1931

With its short straights and easy bends, Clapton was one of the fastest greyhound tracks in the country when it opened in 1928. It staged the Scurry Gold Cup, a race that in its heyday matched the prestige of the Derby. The electric hare being trialled here – the first of its kind – turned the sport based on medieval coursing into its modern format. 'Going to the dogs' was especially popular after World War II with working-class males; at one point there were 33 tracks in London, but now, following the demise of Walthamstow in 2008, there are only two (at Wimbledon and Romford). Clapton closed its doors in 1974, to be replaced by a housing estate.

Popperfoto

Screening in Clissold Park 1957

Is it possible that London park life used to be a lot more adventurous in the past? Certainly, in the wake of the hugely successful Festival of Britain in 1951 and its exciting range of outdoor entertainments, attractions such as alfresco restaurants, outdoor ice-skating, lidos and, as seen here, open-air cinema screenings were widespread and very popular – even if the technology was less than cutting edge. For this daytime showing in Stoke Newington's Clissold Park, a rather basic black and white screen seems to have been attached to the back end of a bus, though such limitations haven't diminished the obvious absorption of the young audience.
Fox Photos/Hulton Archive

John Logie Baird 1925

Scottish electrical engineer John Logie Baird intently adjusts his 'televisor', the precursor to the television. Numerous venues in London bore witness to Baird's gradual development of this seemingly primitive contraption. It was Selfridges department store, bizarrely enough, that hosted the first public display of his moving silhouettes in March 1925. A year later, when these outlines had become fully formed images – basically the world's first TV picture – the audience was a group of 50 scientists and a journalist from *The Times*, all crammed into Baird's two-bedroom attic laboratory at 22 Frith Street, W1. A blue plaque marks the building, which now houses famous Soho café Bar Italia.
Hulton Archive

Marc Bolan
1965

Aged 18, Mark Feld is at the birth of his
career, having just landed a record contract
with Decca. It took a few more years,
however, for the diminutive musician from
Hackney to gain any meaningful recognition
with his two-man band, Tyrannosaurus Rex
(helped along by a young DJ called John Peel).
After playing the first free festival at Hyde
Park in 1968, a new line-up, a truncated
name and a scattering of glitter around the
eyes led Bolan and T-Rex to greater heights
in the early '70s. 'T-Rextasy', however, had
died a death before Bolan's fatal car crash
in 1977 on Barnes Common, where there's
a shrine to his memory. There's also a
plaque at his childhood home at 25 Stoke
Newington Common, and another at Golders
Green Crematorium.

Popperfoto

Fireworks lady 1930

Celebrated fireworks company James Pain & Sons lit up the skies of London for thousands of excited families during the 19th and 20th centuries – here an employee shows off the firm's latest creations, including a maltese wheel and various roman candles, in preparation for Bonfire Night 1930. Founded in the 1860s on the Walworth Road, Pain's moved briefly to Brixton and then, in 1877, to Mitcham, where it stayed until the 1960s (south London was something of a pyrotechnic playground: Brock's, Britain's oldest fireworks manufacturer, was based in nearby Sutton). Supplying fireworks for small personal displays and large professional ones ever since, Pain's is still going strong, winning prestigious fireworks competitions and mounting large-scale displays around the world.

FPG/Hulton Archive

The Rossettis 1863

London-born poet and artist Dante Gabriel Rossetti – seen here playing chess with his mother in the garden of his house in Cheyne Walk, Chelsea, watched by his sisters author Maria and poet Christina (left) – was best known as the co-founder of the Pre-Raphaelite Brotherhood. (He was also, rather improbably, a wombat fanatic, and could often be found in the wombat house at London Zoo.) The picture was one of a series of the family, taken on 7 October 1863 by Charles Dodgson, a prolific amateur portait photographer. Dodgson, aka Lewis Carroll, used the hobby as a way to enter higher social circles and developed particularly close links with the Pre-Raphaelite movement.

Lewis Carroll/Hulton Archive

Open-air restaurant 1951

Although many of the gaping holes that German bombers left in London's skyline, and its streets, lasted well after the war had ended, some were put to enterprising use – as seen here at an alfresco restaurant in Arthur Street, near the Monument. Rebuilding the war-torn city was a massive enterprise, and one that many minds turned to, officially and otherwise. The MARS Group of modernist architects (including Wells Coates and Maxwell Fry) came up with a radical scheme that involved demolishing most of the city, while the Royal Academy's Planning Committee, headed by architect Sir Edwin Lutyens, proposed a far-reaching 100-year plan that turned Covent Garden into a national music and drama centre and included a flying bridge between Charing Cross Road and Piccadilly Circus (which would become rectangular).

Harry Todd/Fox Photos/Hulton Archive

Ella and Ronnie 1963

Musician and jazz club owner Ronnie Scott shares a quiet moment with jazz singer Ella Fitzgerald. Born Ronald Schatt in Aldgate, he played in jazz combos from the age of 16, but is best remembered for running Ronnie Scott's Jazz Club in Soho for four decades. He opened the club (with fellow tenor saxophonist Pete King) in Gerrard Street in 1959; in 1965 it moved to larger premises in Frith Street, where it remains to this day. Ella Fitzgerald is just one of the hundreds of luminaries to have performed there. As club host, Ronnie was famous for his appalling jokes – 'Why don't you all hold hands and see if you can contact the living?' (to the audience) being one regularly used line.

Asher/Express

Cary Grant 1934

Westminster's Caxton Hall was the scene of many a celebrity hitch in its 100 years – Joan Collins, Peter Sellers, Barry Gibb, Ringo Starr, Sir John Mills and Yehudi Menuhin all got married there – but they don't come much bigger than Cary Grant (born Archibald Leach), who wed Hollywood actress Virginia Cherrill there on 9 February 1934. For Grant, it would be the second of five marriages, for Cherrill the second of four; the couple divorced just over a year later. The registry office would last much longer, until 1979. Caxton Hall's impressive history also includes a 1908 Women's Parliament convened by the suffragettes, wartime speeches by Winston Churchill, the 1940 assassination of Sir Michael O'Dwyer (in revenge for the Amritsar massacre 20 years earlier) and, at a meeting in 1967, the formation of the National Front. The building now houses luxury flats.
Popperfoto

Skinhead and punk 1979, 1977

While skinheads and punks shared some visual codes – bleached denim, home-made slogans, tight jeans (though their hairstyles couldn't have been more different) – they were often at polar opposites in terms of their political beliefs. Despite a love of Jamaican dancehall music such as ska, rocksteady and reggae, many 1970s skins were violent, racist nationalists and fascists, with ties to the National Front, whereas the leftist punk movement was determinedly anti-racist, as evidenced by events like the huge Rock Against Racism concert at Victoria Park in 1978. The two groups coexisted warily and often clashed, particularly at 2 Tone concerts, where bands such as the Specials drew both ska-loving skins and anarchist punks.

Iain McKell

Chris Moorhouse/Hulton Archive

Queuing for fuel 1947

An unusually harsh winter and a severe fuel crisis brought about by labour and rolling stock shortages saw housewives queuing for hours to collect their week's coal supply – prams were the ideal vehicle – from the Gas Light & Coke Company's depot in Nine Elms, Vauxhall. So severe was the fuel crisis that earlier the same month (February) domestic cutbacks and a three-day working week in industry had been imposed by Clement Attlee's Labour government, and many iron plants were forced to close for short periods as they exhausted their fuel supplies. Things slowly improved in the post-war years, and the growing appeal of natural gas finally saw the demise of the depot, which was replaced in 1974 by the largest and most important wholesale horticultural market in the country, New Covent Garden Market.

Harry Todd/Fox Photos/Hulton Archive

John Christie 1953

Notorious London serial killer John Reginald Halliday Christie hides his face as he leaves West London Police Court after being accused of killing his wife at 10 Rillington Place (now Ruston Close) in Ladbroke Grove. The bodies of six women were found at the house and Christie was eventually convicted of all six murders and hanged at Pentonville Prison. Two years earlier, Timothy Evans had been executed for killing his own wife and child at the same address, with Christie a principal witness at the trial, but when Christie confessed to those murders, it played a vital part in bringing to an end, in 1965, the death penalty for murder in Britain. Evans received a posthumous pardon a year later. The 1971 film *10 Rillington Place*, with Richard Attenborough as a terrifyingly blank Christie, brilliantly dramatised the chilling story.

Norman Potter/Hulton Archive

Smithfield Market 1953

Meat has been traded at Smithfield Market for over 800 years, and it's the only wholesale market to have stayed in its original central London site. Here, vendors in traditional white butchers' coats take part in the Christmas turkey auction, still an annual event. Before World War II, goose or beef were more common features of the Christmas table, with turkey considered a luxury. This changed with the introduction of intensive turkey farming in the late 1940s, which dramatically cut prices – though, with food rationing still in place in 1953, the auction was packed with bargain hunters and last-minuters. The current Poultry Market, with its enormous concrete dome, was built in the 1960s after the original – designed by Victorian architect Sir Horace Jones (also responsible for Billingsgate and Leadenhall Markets) – was destroyed by fire.

Topical Press Agency/Hulton Archive

Julien Temple
1979

Director Julien Temple was raised on a
north London council estate by his posh but
left-wing parents, and he's claimed that his
father would rather have seen him working
in the Ford car factory than take up his place
at university. He has a long list of film and
music video credits to his name, among them
The Great Rock and Roll Swindle (1980,
and the first of several documentaries he's
made about the Sex Pistols), and *Absolute
Beginners* (1986). The latter, a musical based
on the book about 1950s London by Colin
MacInnes, was criticised in the UK when it
was released, but had more of a following
in the States and led to work in Hollywood.
More recently, Temple has returned to rock
documentary, covering Glastonbury, Joe
Strummer and, in 2008, filming Madness
in concert at the Hackney Empire.

Janette Beckman/Redferns

Hampstead Heath Fair 1892

The 791 acres of rolling grassland and woods that make up Hampstead Heath, now dotted with man-made attractions including three bathing ponds and 14 listed structures, have long been a place of rest and recreation for weary Londoners. No more so than in the 19th century, when daytrippers came in their hordes, drawn by the poetic praise of Shelley and the mesmerising landscapes of Constable, and from 1860 transported by train to the newly opened Hampstead Heath station. By Easter 1892, when this photo was taken, the Heath was attracting up to 100,000 visitors for the regular bank holiday fairs – so dense were the crowds around the station over this particular Easter holiday that nine people were crushed to death as they tried to escape from a storm on the evening of 18 April.

General Photographic Agency/Hulton Archive

The Crazy Gang 1955

Music hall and royal family favourites the Crazy Gang reigned supreme in English comedy from the 1930s to the '50s. The group featured the talents of (left to right) Jimmy Nervo, Teddy Knox, Bud Flanagan, Charlie Naughton and Jimmy Gold, seen here performing at the Victoria Palace Theatre. While all were well known in their own right, it was Bud Flanagan, one half of the duo Flanagan and Allen, who was probably the most famous – he can still be heard today warbling 'Who do you think you are kidding, Mr Hitler?' over the opening credits of the still popular TV sitcom *Dad's Army*. Born Chaim Reuben Weintrop to immigrant Polish Jews in Whitechapel, Flanagan retained a close connection with the East End throughout his life; a blue plaque marks the house he was born in at 12 Hanbury Street.

Houston Rogers/Hulton Archive

Paul Nash
1944

Born in London in 1899, Paul Nash studied at
the Slade and taught at the Royal College of
Art. As well as earning fame for the ineffable
Englishness of his landscapes, he was also
a promoter of avant-garde styles; in 1933
he established Unit One, a group of artists
informed by abstraction and surrealism, which
counted Henry Moore and Barbara Hepworth
among its members. Nash wanted to reach
an audience beyond the conventional gallery-
goers, and his employment as an official war
artist in both World Wars helped him achieve
that. The painting he's working on here,
Landscape of the Vernal Equinox (III), is now
owned by the National Galleries of Scotland.
Picture Post/Hulton Archive

Eartha Kitt
1951

Cabaret singer Eartha Kitt, performing at the Churchill Club, Mayfair, aged just 24. Born on a cotton plantation in South Carolina, she was discovered by Orson Welles in Paris just months before this photo was taken; he cast her as Helen of Troy in his production of *Dr Faustus*, and described her as 'the most exciting woman in the world'. She spent a lot of time performing in Europe after she was blacklisted by President Lyndon Johnson following an anti-Vietnam War outburst at a White House luncheon in 1968. In a long career, she appeared in many films, plays and TV programmes, but she's best remembered as the seductive voice behind such songs as 'Santa Baby' and 'I Want to be Evil'.

Haywood Magee/Picture Post/Hulton Archive

Crippen trial 1910

In August 1910 a huge crowd gathered outside the Old Bailey – 4,000 had applied for only 80 tickets to attend the trial – to see if American-born Dr Hawley Harvey Crippen would be convicted of the murder of his wife Cora, aka music hall singer Belle Elmore. It was claimed he had killed, dismembered and buried her in the cellar of their house in 39 Hilldrop Crescent, Holloway. Crippen and his mistress had fled by boat to Canada, but were famously, and dramatically, captured thanks to a wireless telegram sent by the ship's captain. The jury took 27 minutes to find Crippen guilty; he was hanged at Pentonville Prison in November. The following year, his place in criminal history was assured when his wax figure went on display at Madame Tussaud's Chamber of Horrors; nearly 100 years later, it's still there.

Topical Press Agency/Hulton Archive

Coronation crowds 1911

The lower classes' once deferential attitudes towards peers and the aristocracy were changing fast when King George V succeeded to the throne in 1911. But Londoners still lined the streets in their thousands to see the coronation procession on 22 June; those who couldn't get the day off excitedly watched proceedings from workplace windows. While the Liberal government was committed to curbing the legislative powers of peers and changing a system that benefited the upper classes at the expense of the poor, royalty, aristocrats and the working classes alike would be united three years later when Britain went to war with Germany, an event that would see George, cousin to Kaiser Wilhelm of Germany, abandon the Teutonic-sounding name of Saxe-Coburg-Gotha for the more English 'Windsor'.

Topical Press Agency/Hulton Archive

AV Roe 1910

Posing confidently beside one of his earliest aeroplanes, Alliot Verdon Roe looks every inch the successful aviator. As indeed he was: in 1908 he had been the first Englishman to make a powered flight (although it wasn't officially recognised at the time) and, in 1909, had designed and built his own triplane and then flown it across Walthamstow Marshes – a blue plaque on a railway arch marks the site of his workshop. Such achievements had been aided by meetings with the Wright brothers, the £75 prize money he'd won in a *Daily Mail* model plane competition – and Roe's unwavering optimism. The 504 training biplane made by his aircraft manufacturing company, Avro, was a key player in World War I.
Time Life Pictures/Mansell

Heath Robinson 1930

Cartoonist, illustrator and humorist William Heath Robinson works on a series of decorative panels for ocean liner SS *Empress of Britain* in his studio. Born into a family of artists in Islington in 1872, he specialised in illustrations of complex, implausible or hare-brained contraptions (usually involving excessive use of ropes and pulleys), which were hugely popular – particularly those accompanying the Professor Branestawm children's books. His name has subsequently become a byword for any form of cobbled-together machinery. As a tribute to his madcap creativity one of the codebreaking machines built at Bletchley Park in World War II was named 'Heath Robinson'.
Popperfoto

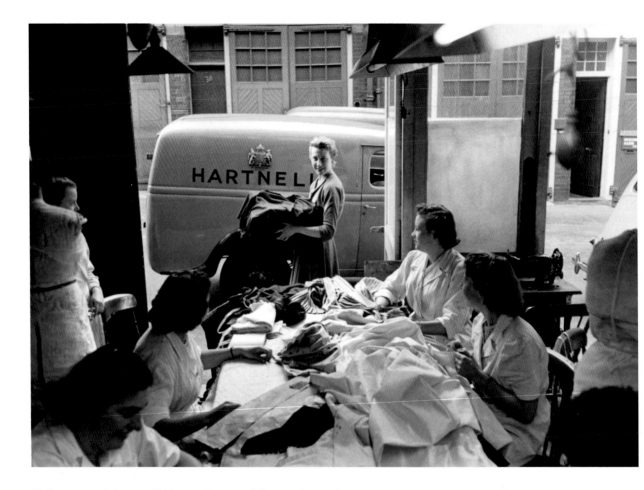

Norman Hartnell 1953

Seamstresses working in Norman Hartnell's Mayfair salon watch as the Queen's coronation dress is taken for delivery to Buckingham Palace, prior to her coronation on 2 June. The dress, here seen covered in black muslin for protection, was made of white satin, embroidered with the emblems of Commonwealth countries in appropriate colours, and was Hartnell's most celebrated commission. Best known as the royal dressmaker (he also created the Queen's wedding dress and continued designing for her and her mother for most of his career), the Streatham-born designer had little impact on mass fashion, but was instrumental in establishing London as a centre of couture. He's commemorated with a blue plaque at 26 Bruton Street, where he lived and worked from 1935 to 1979.

Haywood Magee/Picture Post/Hulton Archive

Silver Jubilee 1977

A wave of patriotic fervour swept the capital during the summer of 1977 in celebration of the Queen's Silver Jubilee. Union flags, bunting and party hats came out in force – as seen here at the Aintree estate in Fulham – as street parties, the like of which hadn't been seen since the end of World War II, were held up and down the land on 7 June, the official anniversary. The same day, the Sex Pistols were arrested while trying to sing their alternative national anthem, 'God Save the Queen', from a boat on the Thames. Released the previous month, the song's controversial lyrics prompted an immediate airplay ban from the BBC, inevitably resulting in it shooting up the singles charts. It peaked at number two, although rumours persist that it was deliberately kept off the top spot to avoid causing offence.

Central Press/Hulton Archive

Rat catcher 1939

A rat catcher, with two ferrets and faithful jack russell, lays out the spoils of his trade on the tracks outside Euston Station. Rats were a major problem during World War II and rat catchers were in great demand, with the rodents sold on to dog breeders. Payment was high as the profession was risky: bites were common and the danger of disease high. A hundred years earlier, rat catchers were employed for a different purpose: to trap live rats for use in rat-baiting, a hugely popular sport in which specially bred dogs were released into a pit full of rats, with punters taking bets on the number killed. In *London Labour and the London Poor*, Victorian journalist Henry Mayhew described a rat-killing match at a pub and interviewed Jack Black, 'the Queen's rat-catcher' – who had a sideline breeding coloured rats to sell as pets to young ladies.

Harry Todd/Fox Photos/Hulton Archive

Toy cars in Hackney 1968

Workers at the Lesney Products factory in Hackney check the quality of finished die-cast toys on an assembly line. Lesney, best known for its Matchbox series of model vehicles, employed around 3,000 people as its toys increased in popularity from the late 1940s. The firm's first major success came in 1953 with a miniature version of the Queen's Coronation Coach, which sold a million; by the end of the '60s, Lesney was pumping out an impressive 100 million Matchbox cars per year. Widely considered to be an exemplary employer by its workers, the company eventually succumbed to the pressures of competition from cheaper manufacturers overseas and went into receivership in 1982, leaving a large hole in the local economy.

Chris Ware/Keystone/Hulton Archive

Knocking-up in Hoxton
1929

Charles Nelson does a spot of 'knocking-up' in Hoxton, as he had been doing for 25 years when this picture was taken. The profession, which involved rattling a long cane with stiff wires attached to it against bedroom windows as a wake-up call, began in earnest with the arrival of the Industrial Revolution, when large numbers of employees needed to get up early but couldn't afford expensive new inventions like alarm clocks. Knocker-uppers, as they were known, were usually men, but in later years women took to the profession too; in the 1930s Mrs Molly Moore claimed to have been the last knocker-up in Britain, using a long rubber tube to shoot dried peas at her clients' windows.

J Gaiger/Topical Press Agency/Hulton Archive

Peter Blake
1958

At the age of 26, the fledgling prince of British Pop Art already sports his trademark beard as he hangs his picture *On the Balcony* in preparation for the Five Painters exhibition at the Institute of Contemporary Arts. The painting, deemed to be one of the iconic pictures of the Pop Art movement, now belongs to the Tate. Claiming that he 'wanted to make an art that was the visual equivalent of pop music', Blake has had a life-long association with the world of rock and pop. A keen Elvis fan, friend of Ian Dury (his one-time student) and designer of album covers for Band Aid, Oasis and Paul Weller, he's still best known (much to his chagrin) as the cover designer of the Beatles album *Sgt Pepper's Lonely Hearts Club Band* – for which he was paid a one-off fee of £200.

Harry Todd/Fox Photos/Hulton Archive

Denis Compton 1953

Unusually, Denis Compton was a double-sided sporting hero, playing at professional level in cricket (for Middlesex) and football (for Arsenal). He also appeared for England in both disciplines, but cricket was his forte; in one glorious record-breaking season, in 1947, he amassed a total of 3,816 runs including 18 centuries. He's seen here leaving the field at the Oval, alongside his batting partner Bill Edrich, having won the fifth Test against Australia: the previous four Tests had been drawn, so England recovered the Ashes – in coronation year, no less – for the first time since 1934. Compton was notoriously forgetful, both on and off the field. At his 70th birthday celebrations in London he was persuaded to take a phone call from a lady who had heard about the dinner: 'Denis, it's me, your mother. You're not 70, you're only 69.'

Central Press/Hulton Archive

Workers at Unilever House 1931

Health and safety regulations were obviously less of an issue in 1931, when construction workers on Unilever House nonchalantly took their tea break atop the half-finished structure's girders. Sited on Victoria Embankment at the northern end of Blackfriars Bridge, the building's curving neo-classical façade is still an eye-catching landmark and it remains Unilever's headquarters. It was Grade II listed in 1977, though the rear extension added in 2007 has caused controversy for blocking the view towards St Paul's Cathedral. The 1864 rail bridge visible in the background no longer exists; it became too weak for modern trains and was demolished in the 1980s – only the red-painted piers remain.
Fox Photos/Hulton Archive

Harold Pinter 1985

One of the most influential playwrights of his generation, Harold Pinter was born and grew up in Hackney. He is photographed here in the study of the Holland Park home he shared with Lady Antonia Fraser. His early experiences of the Blitz – 'the life and death intensity' – and feelings of loss and loneliness on his evacuation were said to have been profound influences, and feature heavily in his work. Pinter was also a poet, actor, director, screenwriter, Nobel prize-winner and obsessive cricket fan. And an outspoken political activist: he became a conscientious objector at 18 and while he'd been 'chuffed to the bollocks' when Tony Blair came to power, by the advent of the invasion of Iraq was describing him as 'a war criminal and murderer'. He died on Christmas Eve 2008 and is buried in Kensal Green Cemetery.

Gemma Levine/Hulton Archive

Balloon factory in Highbury
1951

Workers at the Spencer Brothers balloon factory in Highbury hold aloft one of their creations. The factory produced all sorts and sizes of inflatables, from standard party balloons to the huge observation balloons used during World War II. It was run by Ena Spencer, the great-grand-daughter of pioneering aeronaut Edward Spencer. Born in 1799 in Barnsbury, he practised as a solicitor and became a balloon-maker as well as a parachutist and balloonist, making his first flight on 28 May 1836 from Surrey Zoological Gardens in Kennington. Members of the Spencer family dominated all matters aeronautical in Britain for generations, and Ena followed in the family tradition, first riding in a balloon as a baby and later gaining renown for her triple-parachute jumps.

Fox Photos/Hulton Archive

Berwick Street market 1933

There has been a market in Soho's Berwick Street since the 1700s, though it wasn't officially recognised as such until the turn of the 20th century. By 1933, when this shot was taken, a large number of the stalls and shops sold tailoring and dressmaking wares – drapers, milliners, trimmings vendors, lace and silk dealers and costumiers all plied their trade here, many of them Jewish immigrants from Poland and Russia. The market is much reduced today, but remains the only fruit and veg market in central London; the stalls dealing in fur coats and stoles have long gone, though many of the shops still specialise in fabrics, especially silk.
Fox Photos/Hulton Archive

Harry Gordon Selfridge 1910

Anglo-American industrialist Harry Gordon Selfridge gets on with work shortly after his shop at the 'wrong' end of Oxford Street opened in 1909. The man credited with coining the phrase 'the customer is always right' revolutionised the way the British public thought about shopping – his new department store turning what was once a chore into a hugely enjoyable leisure activity. After a long and successful career, Selfridge was finally undone by wine, women and the Great Depression and was ousted by the executive board and forced to retire – at which point Selfridge's became Selfridges. In his penurious dotage the retail genius frequently made trips to the store that bore his name, on one ignoble occasion nearly being arrested for vagrancy as he stood outside. He died in Putney in 1947.

Hulton Archive

John Betjeman 1974

Poet Laureate, writer, broadcaster and all-round national treasure Sir John Betjeman was born in Highgate in 1906 into the Betjemann family (one 'n' was dropped during World War I to make the name less Germanic). A life-long railway fan – he recorded a series of films for the British Transport Films Unit – and lover of Victorian architecture, he led campaigns to save Euston station's Doric Arch (a failure) and the neo-gothic facade of St Pancras station (a success); a statue of the scruffily dressed poet, gazing upwards with billowing coat and hand on hat, was unveiled at St Pancras after the station's revamp in 2007. His London home for many years, 43 Cloth Fair, near Smithfields Market, is now a Landmark Trust property and can be rented out.

Graham Wood/Evening Standard

Evacuees 1941

Fearing immediate bombing raids on the outbreak of war, an extraordinary three million people, mainly children, were transported from urban areas to the countryside during the first four days of September 1939. Operation Pied Piper was, and still is, the largest ever migration of people within Britain. But the bombs never arrived – this was the period of the Phoney War – and five months later almost 60 per cent had returned home. Many were evacuated again when the Blitz started in earnest that autumn. Although some journalists' rose-tinted views contributed to a skewed stereotypical image of street urchins skipping happily off to the country to lodge like kings in rural idylls – often a far cry from the grim reality of life in a strange place separated from family and friends – these children do indeed look like they are off on a summer holiday.
Keystone/Hulton Archive

Baseball at Wembley 1924

The roots of the game known as America's National Pastime are British, with games such as stoolball serving as direct antecedents of what eventually grew into baseball. As if to repay the favour, various American teams toured the UK playing exhibition games in the late 19th and early 20th centuries, trying to spread the glory of their sport in what amounts to a gentle early example of US cultural imperialism. Several professional leagues did spring up, but most Brits remained resolutely unconverted. The batter here – during a match between the Chicago White Sox and New York Giants – is Ray Schalk, who five years earlier had been one of the few incorruptible members of the White Sox team that conspired to throw the World Series. The tale is told in Eliot Asinof's book *Eight Men Out*, later made into a movie by John Sayles.

Mark Rucker/Transcendental Graphics

Humphrey Lyttelton
1949

The late 1940s saw the rise of jazz revivalism in Britain, with music from 1920s New Orleans regaining popularity. Self-taught trumpeter 'Humph' Lyttelton, photographed at the London Jazz Club at 100 Oxford Street for a *Picture Post* feature, was central to this revival; shows by his eight-piece band were always sell-outs. Lyttelton, whose magnetic stage presence was well documented, was also a successful cartoonist (he studied at Camberwell College of Arts after schooling at Eton and service in World War II) and a much-loved radio broadcaster: he presented the hugely popular BBC Radio 4 comedy panel show *I'm Sorry I Haven't a Clue* from 1972 until his death in 2008, as well as BBC Radio 2's *The Best of Jazz*.

Charles Hewitt/Picture Post/Hulton Archive

Hackney Marshes allotments 1930

This 'food scramble' poster asking Hackney residents to sign a petition if they wanted to keep their means of independent food production alive will resonate with all the plotholders who fought unsuccessfully in 2007 to save nearby Hackney Wick's Manor Garden allotments from the London Development Agency's Olympics 2012 plans. Back in the 1930s, the Hackney and District Smallholders' Society might have had more success (and certainly more hares). Established during World War I to run the borough's hugely popular allotment scheme, the HDSS started out with applications for 90 plots; a year later they had 4,328 allotments, many of them on land at Hackney Marshes.
General Photographic Agency/Hulton Archive

Prohibition march 1917

Children carry banners at a rally in west London in support of Prohibition. Although various temperance organisations had been campaigning for a ban on alcohol in Britain since the 1830s, it was the advent of World War I that had the most direct effect. The Defence of the Realm Act of 1914, a notably sweeping piece of legislation, prohibited and limited a huge number of activities, from flying kites to lighting bonfires, and gave the government powers to censor the press and imprison without trial. It also restricted pub opening times to between noon and 3pm and 6.30pm and 9.30pm. Sugar is mentioned on the banners because it was a rationed substance during the war.
Topical Press Agency/Hulton Archive

Bert Hardy 1955, 1953

One of Britain's greatest photojournalists, Bert Hardy was born in Webber Street, Southwark in 1913. He started out with a second-hand Leica, working for a Fleet Street press agency, before becoming chief photographer at *Picture Post* in 1941, where he remained until the magazine's demise in 1957. He covered an amazing array of subjects in his time – fire-fighting during the Blitz, the liberation of Bergen-Belsen concentration camp, Hollywood stars, Princess Elizabeth's wedding, West End shows, wrestling matches – but is best known for his picture essays charting life in London's poorer areas, including the Docks, the East End and the Elephant (the area he grew up in). These photos were both shot for *Picture Post*: Collins Music Hall (above) in Islington was never published; the other was for a 1953 article entitled 'What Makes Piccadilly'.

Bert Hardy/Hulton Archive

Mahatma Gandhi 1930

Social campaigner and soon-to-be leader of the Labour Party George Lansbury visits Gandhi at Kingsley Hall, the community centre and children's nursery in Bow where the Mahatma stayed during his visit to London for the Round Table Conference in 1931 to discuss Indian home rule. One of the centre's workers, Lylie Valentine, recounted that 'when he arrived, I think all the people in east London waited outside to see him… besides doing his work with the government, he spent a lot of time with us. He visited the nursery school and all the children called him Uncle Gandhi.' Besides politicians, Gandhi's visitors while staying at the hall included Charlie Chaplin, and the Pearly Queen and King of East London. Kingsley Hall is now the headquarters for the Gandhi Foundation.

Hulton Archive

Cassius Clay 1963

Young American heavyweight boxer Cassius Clay lies on his hotel bed in London, holding up five fingers in a prediction of how many rounds it will take him to defeat British boxer Henry Cooper. Clay did some sightseeing, declaring Buckingham Palace 'a swell pad', and jogged in Hyde Park, distributing postcards of himself to bemused bystanders. When he entered Wembley Arena on the night of 18 June, wearing a cardboard crown and a cape emblazoned with the words 'The Greatest', a star-studded, 55,000-strong crowd – who had not taken kindly to Clay's arrogant pre-fight bluster and disrespectful approach to Cooper – roared their support for 'Hen-ery'. The bloody, brutal clash that ensued was ended by the referee in, yes, round five.

Les Trievnor/Hulton Archive

Prefab housing 1947

Britain faced a massive housing shortage at the end of World War II: building had come to a virtual stop during the war, and German bombers had destroyed millions of homes – in London alone more than 400,000 houses were flattened or severely damaged, and another two million slightly damaged. Winston Churchill's 1944 Temporary Housing Programme aimed to plug the gap quickly and cheaply. Thus the prefab was born, and enthusiastically embraced by families who loved the large, bright rooms and fitted kitchens and bathrooms, a pleasant alternative to the cramped and damp terrace houses they had come from. By 1949 more than 156,600 prefabs had been thrown up. Very few remain, though the Excalibur estate in Catford still holds the largest number of post-war prefabs in Britain: 187 houses and a tin-roofed church. In 2009 six of the houses were granted Grade II listed status.

Pat English/Time Life Pictures

Pearly king and banker
1933

An unlikely encounter between Montagu Collet Norman, governor of the Bank of England, and the (unnamed) Pearly King of Hackney, who's selling roses for charity. Norman was always a dapper dresser (though he seems to have met his match here), usually adorned with 'a soft felt hat, bow necktie and a superbly pugnacious goatee', according to *Time* magazine in 1927. He steered the Bank through the hardship years after the Great War, the 1929 stockmarket crash, the abandoning of the gold standard, and most of World War II until retiring in 1944 at the age of 73. Not everyone was a fan. Socialist politician Harold Laski complained in 1940: 'Britain has been conquered only twice in its history. The first time was by William the Norman in 1066 and the second by Montagu the Norman in 1931.'

Topical Press Agency/Hulton Archive

VE Day crowd 1945

On 8 May 1945 crowds on Whitehall celebrate Victory in Europe, after hearing Prime Minister Winston Churchill tell the people of Britain 'This is your victory'. After almost six years of war, the fight in Europe was finally over (fighting in the Far East against Japan continued until 15 August). After his speech, Churchill made his way to the Houses of Parliament; his car was more or less pushed the length of Whitehall by the sheer force of the crowd. For the rest of the day, people flooded into central London and, as night fell, fairly decorous festivities gave way to noisier, more excitable celebrations in which drink flowed, fireworks exploded and complete strangers linked arms and danced in the street.

Popperfoto

Baby in a cage
1934

Why didn't this catch on? In 1934, Poplar borough council in east London was concerned that the youthful inhabitants of local tenements weren't getting enough fresh air and sunshine, and this was their solution: a ramshackle, chicken-wire cage sticking out of a fourth-floor window. At least the cherubic occupant seems oblivious to the fact that there's a deadly drop just beneath his toes. According to www.british-history.ac.uk, a website that documents the architectural history of just about every street in London, 12 of these south-facing 'baby balconies' were installed on Collins and Commodore Houses just off Poplar High Street. The experiment didn't last long: unsurprisingly, the London County Council rejected the idea on safety grounds.

Fox Photos/Hulton Archive

Festival of Britain 1951

Despite appearances to the contrary, this is, happily, not a torchlit procession by the Ku Klux Klan during the Festival of Britain – that much-lauded exhibition and extravaganza on London's South Bank designed to give Britons a sense of recovery and progress following the war. According to the Festival of Britain Society, it was a fancy dress parade, held at the Festival Pleasure Gardens in Battersea. We think it probably represented the kind of Holy Week processions that are typical of southern Spain. These processions feature *nazarenos*, who wear long habits and distinctive pointed hoods and carry long candles; the KKK used them as the model for their own robes. Such simple garments would have been easy to assemble in the early 1950s, when materials for fancy dress costumes were in short supply.
Keystone/Hulton Archive

Gladstone on the tube 1862

On this momentous day in London's history – 12 May 1862 – William Ewart Gladstone (front row, near right), then chancellor of the exchequer, travels with directors and engineers of the Metropolitan Railway Company on an inspection tour of the world's first tube line. The tunnels had been built using the cut-and-cover method, which involved carving out a deep trench, building side walls and a roof and backfilling the ground surface. Although it was expensive, disruptive and slow work, the four-mile line between Bishop's Road in Paddington and Farringdon Street in the City had taken a mere two years and three months to build. It would be another seven months before the line officially opened, when an impressive 38,000 passengers travelled on it. Nowadays, annual passenger numbers are closer to 38 million.

Hulton Archive

Newspaper sellers 1936

Vendors vigorously selling papers containing the football final results on the Thames Embankment, on 12 January 1936. At that time there was room for several evening newspapers in London – the *Evening News* (established 1881), the *Evening Standard* (1859) and the *Star* (1788) – and all enjoyed buoyant sales. The *Evening News* had the highest circulation figures during the 1930s, regularly selling in excess of 800,000 copies, more than its rivals combined. Newspaper sales declined as other means of rapid communication developed; the *Star* folded in 1957, and in 1980 a struggling *Evening News* was merged with the *Evening Standard* (though the name remains on the front page of the *Standard* to this day).
HF Davis/Topical Press Agency/Hulton Archive

Screaming Lord Sutch
1988

From 1963 when he first contested the Stratford upon Avon by-election caused by the resignation of John Profumo, Hampstead-born rock musician David Sutch, better known as 'Screaming Lord Sutch, 3rd Earl of Harrow', was a welcome figure in British political life, providing a light-hearted distraction in his flamboyant suits and trademark top hat. Ultimately, however, Sutch – and the Official Monster Raving Loony Party he founded in 1983 – failed to make any real impact, with the possible exception of the 1990 Bootle by-election, when his success in gaining more votes than David Owen contributed to the disbanding of the SDP. Hundreds of mourners turned out for his funeral in 1999, which featured a motorbike cavalcade and a rendition of Chuck Berry's 'Roll Over Beethoven'.
Popperfoto

Café de Paris 1953

A host of Hollywood bigwigs – including Humphrey Bogart, Lauren Bacall, James Mason, Josephine Baker and David O Selznick – enjoy a night out at the glamorous Café de Paris on Coventry Street, just off Piccadilly Circus. Opened in 1924 by impresario Harry Foster, the club enjoyed early success thanks to the patronage of the Prince of Wales (later Edward VIII), and was a popular venue for Cole Porter to try out new songs. It remained open during World War II until it took a direct hit on 8 March 1941: two landmines fell through the roof, destroying the dancefloor and killing 84 people, including band leader Ken 'Snakehips' Johnston, who was on stage at the time. The Café bounced back after the war, again attracting royalty (Princess Margaret was a regular), but went into decline in the following decades and was turned into a dance hall before being reborn in the mid 1990s.

John Heddon/Express/Hulton Archive

London Olympics 1908

Despite perfecting her dismount from the pommel horse, this Danish gymnast didn't get the chance to win a medal at the 1908 Olympics: women's gymnastics remained an exhibition event until the 1928 Games in Amsterdam. This was the first time the Olympics were held in London; the main site, in White City, was shared with the Franco-British Exhibition, which at the time was considered the more important event. The Games saw some notable firsts. Tug-of-war made its only appearance as an Olympic sport; two teams of British policemen contested the final, with the City of London force beating Liverpool. It was also the first (and last) time that Britain topped the medal table, winning 99 more medals than its nearest rival, the United States – which may have been why there were numerous complaints about favouritism, chauvinism and poor refereeing. The weather was dismal too.

Topical Press Agency/Hulton Archive

Jellied eel stall 1951

A traditional dish of the English working class, jellied eels date back to the 18th century, their association with London's East End being rooted in the one-time abundance of eels caught in nets along the banks of the Thames. While oysters, originally another cheap and plentiful food source for the capital's poorer classes, have gone on to better themselves, eels, particularly in jellied form (created by boiling chopped eels in stock with spices, the gelatinous nature of the flesh creating the jelly), have remained resolutely downmarket. Although a lot less popular than they were in the 1950s, they can still be found at seafood stalls and pie and mash shops (mainly in east and south-east London), where they're eaten hot or cold, doused in spiced vinegar.

Picture Post/Hulton Archive

Beatrice and Sidney Webb
1929

The Webbs – pictured here outside the Royal Academy of Arts – were social reformers who sowed the seeds of Britain's welfare state with their 1909 *Minority Report* for the Royal Commission on the Poor Law. The couple, who are often referred to jointly owing to their active professional life together, co-authored several books, including the *History of Trade Unionism* (1894). They were founding members of the Fabian Society, founders of the London School of Economics and members of the Labour Party, whose constitution Sidney played a central role in creating. Although much of their work was rejected by the Liberal government of the day, their writings were instrumental in forming contemporary political thought and practice. Their support for Stalin's Soviet Union, however, garnered criticism, most famously from HG Wells. They both died in the 1940s and their ashes are interred in Westminster Abbey.

Topical Press Agency/Hulton Archive

Weller and Townshend
1980

This shot of Jam co-founder Paul Weller and British rock icon and modfather Pete Townshend of the Who outside the Marquee Club on Wardour Street exhibits the trademark style of music photographer Janette Beckman; it appeared under the tag 'The Punk and the Godfather' on the cover of *Melody Maker*. London-born Beckman honed her skills with the emergence of punk, documenting major players such as the Clash and the Sex Pistols as well as lesser-known bands like the Raincoats, and Echo and the Bunnymen. Beckman's skill lay in capturing the scene's energy and youthful exuberance, underpinning wit and insight with a strong narrative. As interest shifted in the early 1980s to hip hop and rap in the US, so did Beckman; she left London for New York in 1982, and has been documenting underground and emerging youth culture in the States ever since.

Janette Beckman

Chelsea Flower Show 1997

The Royal Horticultural Society's floral extravaganza in May is one of the longest-running events on London's social calendar. The first Great Spring Show (the official title) was held in 1862 in Kensington; it moved to the grounds of the Royal Hospital in Chelsea in 1913 and has been there ever since, bar a hiatus during World War II when the War Office requisitioned the land as an anti-aircraft site. These days, nearly 160,000 gardening fanatics turn up each year (numbers are limited by the size of the site and all tickets are sold in advance) to marvel at the outlandish show gardens, get tiddly on expensive champagne and discover the latest developments in spade technology. All sense of decorum vanishes at 4pm on the final day when visitors stampede for cut-price blooms as exhibitors sell off their displays.

Dod Miller

Shipyard in Poplar 1907

This picture marks a moment of decline in London's shipbuilding industry. Founded by Alfred Yarrow in the 1870s, the Yarrow shipyard in Poplar on the Isle of Dogs made hundreds of steam launches and, later, Royal Navy torpedo boats and destroyers (as well as naval boats for other countries including Japan and Greece) until rising labour and land costs forced a move to Scotstoun, Glasgow, in 1908. The year 1907 was a time of uncertainty for the company as it relocated northwards, a process that took two years to complete as thousands of tonnes of equipment and heavy machinery was dismantled and then transported to Scotland. Around 300 local workers also moved north with the firm.
Topical Press Agency/Hulton Archive

Chelsea Pensioners 1938

The bedrooms for 'In-Pensioners' at the Royal Hospital Chelsea have changed little since 1682, when the complex, designed by Sir Christopher Wren, was founded for the 'succour and relief of veterans broken by age and war'. Despite the seeming austerity of the 'berths' (which at the time of this picture consisted simply of a bunk with a radio) more than 300 veterans happily reside in the exclusive retirement home, where perks include a library, bowling green and arts and crafts centre – and tickets to watch Chelsea FC. In March 2009 women were admitted for the first time, as long as they were willing and able to meet the same criteria as their male counterparts: surrender of their army pension, wearing of two uniforms (navy blue 'undress' in the barracks and the famous, more formal scarlet coats outside) and no dependent spouse.

Kurt Hutton/Picture Post/Hulton Archive

Marie Lloyd 1908

Born in Hoxton in 1870, Matilda Alice Victoria Wood began her career as one of the Fairy Bells Minstrels singing temperance songs in local churches. By the time she'd become London's most celebrated music hall entertainer, her songs had got raunchier, with lines such as 'she'd never had her ticket punched before' accompanied by salacious smiles and winks. Her popularity ensured that she could command her own fees for shows, but when less fortunate performers went on strike a sympathetic Lloyd performed on the picket line. Seeing a face she recognised, she shouted: 'Let her through, girls, she'll close the music hall faster than we can'. The singer was Belle Elmore, later murdered by her husband, Dr Crippen. More than 100,000 people attended Lloyd's funeral at Hampstead Cemetery in 1922. A blue plaque marks her former home at 55 Graham Road, E8, and the Hackney Empire's bar is named after her.
Hulton Archive

Winston Churchill 1963

A frail Winston Churchill welcomes spring in Richmond Park by feeding the deer. These were testing times for the 88-year-old statesman, who had taken a long time to recover from a broken leg sustained while holidaying in Paris the previous summer. A few months after this picture was taken, Churchill and his wife were hit hard by tragedy. First came the death of their son-in-law in Spain, then their daughter Diana died from an overdose of sleeping pills. The old man gradually retired from public life as his advisers and family persuaded him to relinquish his seat in the House of Commons, which he eventually did in the summer of 1964. Churchill lived his last few years quietly at 28 Hyde Park Gate, Kensington, and died there on 24 January 1965.

Terry Fincher/Express/Hulton Archive

Climbing Albert Bridge 1926

The elegant Albert Bridge linking Chelsea and Battersea was designed in the 1860s by Rowland Mason Ordish, who conceived it as a rigid suspension bridge soaring up to 400 feet in its centre span, complete with ornate decorative touches such as lanterns and pagodas. By the time this picture was taken, in 1926, it had been modernised and strengthened by Sir Joseph Bazalgette, but since then has changed little, except for a new ice-cream-toned colour scheme in the 1980s. Campaigns over the years led by John Betjeman and Diana Dors have saved it from demolition, making it the only bridge in central London never to have been replaced – and the only one with a pop song named after it: 'Misty Morning, Albert Bridge' by the Pogues.

Fox Photos/Hulton Archive

Tube workers
1937

Workmen are lowered into a deep shaft near
Baker Street to start work on an extension
to the Bakerloo Underground line. Opened
in 1906, the line, which originally ran from
Baker Street to Waterloo Station – the name
'Bakerloo' was apparently coined by a
columnist on the *Evening News* – was soon
extended and then amalgamated with bits
of other tube lines to alleviate congestion
as the network grew. The Underground has
starred in numerous novels, films and
television programmes, but rarely as directly
as in science fiction writer Geoff Ryman's
interactive novel *253 or tube theatre*. The
structure of the piece is based on the premise
that each seven-carriage Bakerloo train has
36 seats, making a total of 252 passengers
plus one driver.

Harry Todd/Fox Photos/Hulton Archive

Sigmund Freud 1938

A seriously ill Sigmund Freud – he died of oral cancer in September 1939 – at his new home in north London, surrounded by some of the ancient figurines he brought with him from Vienna. London provided the father of psychoanalysis with refuge from the Nazis after the German annexation of Austria; he and his family arrived in Hampstead in June 1938. His house at 20 Maresfield Gardens is now the Freud Museum: the study and library have been preserved as he left them, complete with the iconic couch and a collection of almost 2,000 antiquities. His ashes are interred, in a Greek urn from his collection, in the Columbarium at Golders Green Crematorium.

Imagno/Hulton Archive

Don Letts 1977

London-born musician and filmmaker Don Letts, pictured at the Roxy nightclub in Covent Garden. He was resident DJ at the short-lived club (January 1977 to April 1978), and as such is credited with introducing reggae to the punk scene. His first film, *The Punk Rock Movie*, was largely made from Super 8 camera footage he shot while at the club. Letts managed the Slits, founded Big Audio Dynamite with ex-Clash member Mick Jones, and won a Grammy for his documentary on the Clash, *Westway to the World*. He currently presents a weekly show on Saturdays for BBC Radio 6 Music.

Erica Echenberg/Redferns

Paul Martin 1900

Pioneering Victorian photographer Paul Martin eschewed formal portraiture and art photography in favour of a naturalistic documentary style, capturing fascinating casual and candid everyday scenes of Londoners at work, rest and play. Born in France in 1864, he came to London as a child in the wake of the Franco-Prussian war and the Paris Commune. In 1892 he purchased a 'Facile' camera – a new hand-held model, which he disguised as a parcel in order to surreptitiously photograph London life in a way no one else had. As well as these pictures of a sherbert seller on Cheapside and kids enjoying a ride on a elephant in Regent's Park, he snapped organ grinders, bootblacks, match sellers, Billingsgate Market porters, knifegrinders, boys skinny-dipping in the Serpentine and holidaymakers at Hampstead Heath Fair.
Paul Martin/General Photographic Agency/Hulton Archive

Rough Trade 1977

Left-wing Cambridge graduate Geoff Travis (sitting at the counter, far left) came back from a trip to the US in late 1975 with a dream – the music fan envisioned creating a record shop that mirrored the independent spirit of City Lights bookshop in San Francisco. In February 1976, in a tiny shop on Kensington Park Road, he opened the now-legendary Rough Trade. It was a mecca for fans of the burgeoning punk scene, who would stay for hours listening to new music by the likes of the Slits, the Sex Pistols, Jonathan Richman, and Siouxsie and the Banshees, as well as reggae from Jamaican legends such as Lee 'Scratch' Perry and Dr Alimantado. The Rough Trade record label would go on to sign everyone from Stiff Little Fingers and the Smiths to the Strokes and the Libertines, and become a key part of London – and British – musical history.
Erica Echenberg/Redferns

Mandy Rice-Davies and Christine Keeler 1963

Months after details of what came to be known as the Profumo Affair – a scandalous web of sex, politics and espionage – became public, the female leads Mandy Rice-Davies (left) and Christine Keeler leave the Old Bailey on the first day of the trial of Stephen Ward. Ward, a well-connected osteopath, was accused of living off immoral earnings; he had invited Keeler to live in his Wimpole Mews flat, then introduced her to Secretary of State for War Jack Profumo. Of the two women, it was Rice-Davis whose ready wit has stayed in the public mind. When the prosecuting counsel pointed out that Lord Astor denied having an affair with her, she replied, 'Well, he would, wouldn't he?' – a phrase that has become a stock sceptical response in modern argot. She also described her life as 'one slow descent into respectability'.
Keystone/Hulton Archive

Serafina Astafieva and Alicia Markova 1922

Russian princess Serafina Astafieva (at the far right) performed with Diaghilev's Ballet Russes before setting up her own dancing school in Chelsea, where her pupils included Margot Fonteyn, Anton Dolin and Marie Rambert. Diaghilev brought his young protégée Alicia Markova (in the very centre of the picture) for the princess to approve: 'a racehorse' was the teacher's verdict on the young dancer from Finsbury Park. Markova later joined the forerunners of Ballet Rambert and the Royal Ballet and became one of the world's greatest classical ballerinas. Astafieva's studio at 152 King's Road in the well-known artists' colony the Pheasantry (the building was originally used to raise royal game) is now a branch of Pizza Express. A blue plaque commemorates Princess Serafina's time there.

Topical Press Agency/Hulton Archive

Festival planners 1951

Misha Black, James Holland, Ralph Tubbs and Hugh Casson (left to right, shown here in January 1951), together with James Gardner, were the architects and designers responsible for the overall plan of the South Bank site of the 1951 Festival of Britain. It was a huge opportunity, but also a great challenge – an ex-slum site between Westminster and Waterloo bridges had to be transformed into a showcase of 'British Achievement in the Arts, Science and Industry' in just a few years. Of the five, Misha Black had perhaps the greatest impact on London, thanks to his long relationship with London Transport. He designed many iconic posters, as well as the distinctive orange-black-brown-yellow patterned upholstery used on buses and trains, and worked on every aspect of the Victoria line (built 1968-71), from stations to train fittings.
Picture Post/Hulton Archive

Audrey Hepburn
1950

Three years before her appearance alongside Gregory Peck in *Roman Holiday* catapulted her to international stardom, Audrey Hepburn was a struggling singer-dancer in the 'Sauce Piquante' revue at London's Cambridge Theatre. But there must have been something about the fresh-faced 20-year-old – showing early promise as a chic dresser in her checked suit and beret – that made *Picture Post* whisk her off to Kew Gardens and Richmond Park for a photo session with its chief photographer, Bert Hardy. The article was titled 'We take a Girl to look for Spring'. Tulips had a particular resonance for Hepburn; she spent World War II in the Netherlands, where her family faced such hardship that they resorted to making flour out of tulip bulbs.
Bert Hardy/Picture Post/Hulton Archive

Sioux on Hampstead Heath 1925

Walkers on Hampstead Heath on this winter's day must have been bemused to come across this quartet of Sioux Indians, in feathered head-dresses and beaded leather jerkins, sledging in the snow. Though probably not as bemused as the Indians themselves. Members of the 101 Ranch company, the Sioux were in London to participate in Bertram Mills Circus's annual Christmas season at Olympia (a fixture from 1920 and hugely popular, with people queuing round the block for tickets). Wild West shows were common across Europe from the turn of the 20th century until the mid 1930s, with Native Americans presenting stereotyped and romanticised enactments of tribal life, complete with mock fights, dance displays and faux village settings where visitors could browse handicraft stalls.

Fox Photos/Hulton Archive

Italia Conti Academy 1952

Showbiz wannabes practise their moves at the Italia Conti Academy, one of the country's oldest performing arts schools. Founded in 1911 by actress Italia Conti in a basement studio on Great Portland Street, the school now has premises in Clerkenwell and Clapham and offshoots around the country. Stars of stage and screen to have passed through its doors include Noël Coward, Gertrude Lawrence, Anton Dolin, Clive Dunn, Bonnie Langford, Sadie Frost, Wendy Richard and Googie Withers. This photo was taken by Grace Robertson, who broke into the male-dominated world of journalism in the late 1940s, when she submitted work to *Picture Post* under a male pseudonym. Self-taught, she freelanced for the magazine (where she met her husband, photojournalist Thurston Hopkins) from 1950-57.

Grace Robertson/Picture Post/Hulton Archive

Peter Sellers 1956

The first man to appear on the cover of *Playboy* magazine was eight years away from such notoriety when this picture was taken at the comedian's home in Muswell Hill, flanked by *Picture Post* photographer Thurston Hopkins (left) and journalist Bob Muller. At this point Sellers was known for *The Goon Show* and British films *The Ladykillers*, *I'm All Right Jack* and *The Mouse That Roared*. His fame would hit new heights in the 1960s with such gems as *Lolita*, *Dr Strangelove* and *The Pink Panther*, but a troubled life that included violent rages, four marriages, substance abuse, depression and ill-health ended in 1980 when he was just 54 years old. Thurston Hopkins, born in 1913, worked for *Picture Post* from 1950 until it folded in 1957, and is regarded as one of Britain's finest photojournalists.

John Chillingworth/Picture Post/Hulton Archive

Lilian Baylis
1933

London's performing arts scene owes a
lot to Lilian Baylis. She started her career
helping her aunt at the Royal Victoria Coffee
and Music Hall (now the Old Vic), becoming
manager in 1912; instead of simply offering
cheap amusement, along strict temperance
lines, to south London's miserable slum
tenants, Baylis determined to elevate
and educate, putting on a full cycle of
Shakespeare's plays. She then turned her
attentions to the derelict Sadler's Wells,
which reopened in 1931 with a production
of *Twelfth Night* starring John Geilgud and
Ralph Richardson. She helped nurture the
careers of, among others, Alec Guinness,
Laurence Olivier, Edith Evans and Margot
Fonteyn, and by the time of her death in
1937 had also founded the forerunners of
the Royal Ballet, the National Theatre and
the English National Opera.

Sasha/Hulton Archive

Francis Bacon 1970

Through Britain's post-war years and into the 1960s, artist Francis Bacon was to London what Andy Warhol was to New York. Where Warhol had his coterie of creative party animals and the Factory, Bacon was at the heart of a louche and chaotic group of artists and intellectuals, including Lucian Freud, Graham Sutherland, John Deakin and Dan Farson. When they weren't holed up in legendary Soho drinking club the Colony Room, they assessed and documented everything from the shattered psyche of post-war Britain to the repression of homosexuality – something the troubled Bacon knew a good deal about. He arrived in London in 1926 as a naive 17-year-old, but it wasn't until 1961 that he settled in Reece Mews, Kensington, where he lived until his death in 1992.

James Jackson/Hulton Archive

Rosie Newman 1948

Amateur filmmaker and socialite Rosie Newman threads a projector before screening her film *Britain at War* in the appropriately elite setting of the Dorchester hotel. With a taste for up-to-the-minute film technology and a rich father to bankroll the huge amounts of expensive 16mm Kodachrome film she got through, Newman was in some ways well placed to document the war. Her high society contacts gave her rare access to the three armed services – the film features Spitfires in training and preparations for D-Day, as well as scenes in London during the Blitz and victory celebrations in 1946. Now owned by the Imperial War Museum, it's the only full-length colour film made in Britain during the war. Other footage by Newman was shown for the first time in 70 years in the recent BBC television series *The Thirties in Colour*.

Keystone/Hulton Archive

British Empire Exhibition 1924

The 'Whirl of the World' ride – a sedate version of dodgems, it seems – was part of the British Empire Exhibition that ran for two summer seasons in 1924 and 1925, attracting 27 million visitors. The extravaganza was designed to celebrate, showcase and promote trade between Empire countries (58 at the time – only two didn't take part) and in so doing strengthen imperial relations shaken by World War I and burgeoning independence movements. The centrepiece was the 16 buildings representing the Empire's different countries and regions, but there was also an amusement park, an ornamental lake and gardens and a purpose-built bus station. Built from scratch in north London, most of the buildings (many constructed from that most modern of materials, concrete) were meant to be temporary, but the Empire Pool survived to become Wembley Arena and the Empire Stadium lasted until 2002 as Wembley Stadium.

Hulton Archive

Elephants in Docklands 1947

King George V Dock, now home to London City Airport, has seen pretty much every form of cargo come and go – including this post-war consignment of baby elephants. Designed in 1911 to cope with a new era of shipping, the third of the 'Royal' docks (after Albert and Victoria) was state of the art when finally completed in 1921, equipped with high-tech electric cranes and refrigeration facilities, and large enough to accommodate a variety of steamers, container ships and massive passenger liners such as the *Mauretania*. Having survived the voyage halfway round the world from Ceylon (now Sri Lanka) on the steam ship *Arbratus*, these unfortunate infant pachyderms were bound for the less exotic delights of Tom Arnold's Christmas Circus in Harringay.

Popperfoto

Cat Stevens 1967

Budding pop star Cat Stevens leaps over a bollard in Carnaby Street the year his first album, *Matthew and Son*, hit the charts. Born Steven Demetre Georgiou in 1948, he grew up just round the corner, in a flat over the Moulin Rouge café on Shaftesbury Avenue run by his Greek-Cypriot and Swedish parents. His West End childhood – within earshot of the latest musicals, next door to the guitar shops of Denmark Street and near the folk clubs of Soho – sparked a musical career that resulted in international superstardom in the early '70s, after the release of his fourth album, *Tea for the Tillerman*. His decision to quit the music business in 1977, at the height of his fame, and convert to Islam (taking the name Yusuf Islam) was a shock; he didn't return to the pop world until 2006.

John Pratt/Keystone Features/Hulton Archive

Terence Stamp 1967

Born in 1939 in Canal Road, Bow, Terence Stamp became a 1960s icon, as famous for his gorgeous girlfriends as for his acting (and own good looks). The 1967 premiere of *Far from the Madding Crowd*, in which he starred, was held at the Odeon Marble Arch, and Stamp arrived with model Celia Hammond on his arm, even though he was having an off-screen affair with his co-star Julie Christie. Following the break-up of his relationship with supermodel Jean Shrimpton, he disappeared from the scene for over a decade, but returned to his London roots when he played an ex-con hard man in Stephen Frears's 1999 movie *The Limey*. Celia Hammond now runs an animal rescue charity.

Central Press/Hulton Archive

Painting panto heads 1931

Women at the Pytram factory in New Malden, on the outskirts of south-west London, put the finishing touches to the giant papier-mâché heads they have been creating for the 1931 pantomime season. Traditional English panto, complete with ugly sisters, even uglier dames and much cross-dressing, is the bastard offspring of a union between Italian commedia dell'arte and homegrown music hall. It was at its most popular in the 19th century, when music hall comedian Dan Leno set the standard for all subsequent pantomime dames in the role of Mother Goose, complete with bun wig, apron, knitted shawl and buttoned boots; in those days the London panto season ran from Christmas to Easter.
Fox Photos/Hulton Archive

Ian Dury
1980

Sometime *NME* and *Time Out* photographer
David Corio captures punk-funk-rock icon Ian
Dury in concert with his band, the Blockheads,
at the Lyceum. Born in north London and an
ex-Royal College of Art student, Dury formed
his first band, Kilburn and the High-Roads, in
1970, but was at the height of his fame and
creativity in the late '70s, producing Top Ten
hits such as 'Hit Me With Your Rhythm Stick'
and 'Reasons to be Cheerful, Part 3', as well
as the classic 'Sex & Drugs & Rock & Roll'.
Disabled by polio as a child, Dury was to some
extent seen as a role model for other disabled
people – but above all he was a rebel: his
song 'Spasticus Autisticus', commissioned
specially for the International Year of Disabled
Persons in 1981, was banned by the BBC.
David Corio/Michael Ochs Archives

Clare Market
1910

A warren of lanes west of Lincoln's Inn between the Strand and Drury Lane was once Clare Market, a thriving and expanding meat market from the 17th century – and a fetid slum by the time this picture was taken. The area survived the Great Fire of London and contained many wooden buildings until the early 20th century, when it was redeveloped to make way for the Aldwych and Kingsway. Charles Dickens Jr, writing in 1879, said of the market's offerings: 'It is meat, and you take it on faith that it is meat of the ox or sheep; but beyond that you can say nothing… It is a relief to turn from the butchers' shops to the costermongers' barrows.'

Popperfoto

Nancy Astor 1919

Taken as the results of the Plymouth Sutton constituency by-election were read out, this picture records the moment that Nancy Astor won her place in the House of Commons, becoming the first woman MP to take up her seat in Parliament. The daughter of an American slave owner, she came to Britain in 1905 and married 3rd Viscount William Waldorf Astor. Winning by a comfortable majority as the Tory candidate (in what was once her husband's constituency), she was MP for Plymouth Sutton for 26 years until 1945. Renowned not so much as a feminist trail-blazer as for her wit – 'I married beneath me: all women do' – Lady Astor is flanked by her fellow candidates: a grinning WT Gay (Labour) on her right, and Isaac Foot (Liberal – and father of future Labour Party leader Michael) on her left.

Time Life Pictures/Mansell

Tom Jones
1972

Fulfilling what was surely many a housewife's fantasy, Tom Jones takes a ride on a London bus (and smokes a cigar on the top deck) before alighting in… Arizona State Park. Confused? Not if you've seen *The Special London Bridge Special* – a 1972 made-for-TV extravaganza in honour of the rededication of the old London Bridge in Lake Havasu City, Arizona. In one of the more bizarre turns of Welsh crooner Jones's up-and-down career, the musical saw Sir Tom (having been whisked on his double-decker to America) serenade Raquel Welch, watch Engelbert Humperdink jump off the bridge, attend a performance by the Carpenters, and star in a tap routine with Kirk Douglas. Rudolf Nureyev, Terry-Thomas and Charlton Heston also appear. Sadly, no DVD of this work of genius exists.

Central Press/Hulton Archive

Graham Sutherland 1954

Neo-romantic English artist and official World War II artist, Graham Sutherland sits with his unfinished portrait of Winston Churchill, a joint commission by both Houses of Parliament. The ailing prime minister (who retired because of ill health in April 1955) was apparently a difficult subject; it's telling that at this moment in the picture's evolution the great man's head has yet to be painted. Churchill famously loathed the finished picture, apparently remarking that 'It makes me look half-witted, which I ain't'. It was given to him as a present on his 80th birthday and, following his death, destroyed by his wife Clementine. Fortunately, studies of the work remain and can be seen in the National Portrait Gallery.

Baron/Hulton Archive

Coronation fairground
1937

With the unexpected abdication of Edward VIII in 1936 over his relationship with American divorcee Wallis Simpson, the ground was laid for the coronation of his younger brother Albert, as George VI. Committees and councils across the land (and Empire) went into feverish planning of celebrations to mark the event, on 12 May 1937; the first coronation to be watched, by around 10,000 Britons, on the BBC's new-fangled television service. In Camberwell, the council erected a fairground as a treat for the borough's youngsters – one of the towers of nearby Crystal Palace, which had burned down the year before, is visible background left.

William Vanderson/Fox Photos/Hulton Archive

Notting Hill Carnival riot 1976

Notting Hill's West Indian community first hosted a Caribbean-style carnival, with music, dancing and parade, in 1965. Held on the August Bank Holiday weekend, it's now Europe's largest street party and a highlight of London's cultural and tourist calendar – and a peaceful, family affair. Not so in its early years. In 1976 tension between the police and the black community reached boiling point over the use of the 'sus' law that permitted officers to stop-and-search on suspicion alone. Violence exploded after a black youth was arrested for pickpocketing, and a full-blown riot ensued. The police were forced to flee down Portobello Road; more than 100 were taken to hospital, along with 60 festival-goers, and there were scores of arrests. The riot was pivotal in the implementation of the 1976 Race Relations Act, banning racial discrimination.
Evening Standard/Hulton Archive

Pogo sticks in Edmonton 1958

When it comes to toys, where America leads, Britain often follows, as the Taylor quadruplets from Edmonton demonstrate on their pogo sticks. Although the bouncy inventions would never reach the heights of popularity they enjoyed in the US in the 1920s, when they were patented by George Hansburg and the Zeigfeld Follies performed on them, they were much in demand in Britain and remained popular for another three decades. Other faddish toys came and went – some, like the schoolyard favourite 'clackers', two hard plastic balls on strings, were almost immediately banned – but the pogo stick lives on, with a renaissance that's seen the return of both the popular Master Pogo design pictured here and the invention of more extreme sports versions like the Flybar, which can jump to heights of six feet.

George W Hales/Hulton Archive

Albert Pierrepoint
1973

From becoming assistant executioner in 1932
to resigning the post of chief executioner in
1956, Albert Pierrepoint – seen here working
on his memoirs – officially dispatched more
souls than any other Briton in the 20th
century: over 430. He felt he was born to
take on this poisoned chalice: his father
and grandfather had been executioners too.
He was famously reticent, respectful and
efficient throughout his secondary career (he
was a publican by trade). It was said he could
escort a prisoner to the gallows and drop
them to their death in just seven seconds.
Notorious London hangings he oversaw
included those of Derek Bentley, Timothy
Evans (both awarded posthumous pardons),
John Christie, Lord Haw Haw and Ruth Ellis.

Ian Tyas/Hulton Archive

Artists on the Thames 1947

The foreshore of the Thames used to be a hive of activity in days past, what with amateur archaeologists, mudlarks, bathers at the beach next to Tower Bridge – and the Wapping Group of Artists, who spent their Friday evenings in summer on Bankside, sketching the wharves, piers, bridges and ships. *Picture Post* documented the artists' activities just after the war, when they found new inspiration in the city's bomb-damaged skyline; in the foreground is the group's first president, Jack Merriott, a professional landscape and portrait artist whose work featured on numerous British railway posters. The Wapping Group (membership limited to 25) still exists, and remains devoted to outdoor painting, meeting on the river (from Henley to the Medway) from April to September. It holds an annual show at the Mall Galleries, SW1.

Raymond Kleboe/Picture Post/Hulton Archive

Madness 1979

The Invaders changed their name to Madness in 1979 and a quintessential (north) London band were on their way to many years of chart domination, beginning with 'The Prince', a tribute to Prince Buster. Their first gig under the new name was at the Hope & Anchor pub in Islington, and many of their videos were shot in and around the capital – 'Baggy Trousers' at Kentish Town Primary School; 'Cardiac Arrest' on a double-decker bus; and parts of 'House of Fun' in Escapade fancy dress shop on Camden High Street. The band split up in 1986, but reformed in 1992, and since then have staged several Madstock festivals and seen their songs form the basis of two musicals, *One Step Beyond!* and *Our House*.
Kerstin Rodgers/Redferns

Heatwave 1935

Although the summer of 1935 failed to make it into the record books, it was still hot enough for this group of firemen to oblige in a spot of community cooling for local children. London has experienced its fair share of heatwaves, with the legendary summer of 1976 beating them all for longevity. Combined with a severe drought, the mercury remained above 26°C (79°F) for 25 consecutive days, with temperatures reaching a sweltering 32°C (89°F) or above for over a fortnight; the hot weather even provoked parliament to pass a Drought Act and appoint a short-lived Minister for Drought. The country's highest recorded temperature of 38.5°C (101.3°F) was attained at Faversham, Kent, on 10 August 2003.

Hulton Archive

Vibrators at Victoria Station 1964

This picture is not what it might seem. The vibrators being tested by three customers are Foot Vibrating Machines, designed to help stressed commuters relax – though, presumably, only the chap on the left, who has bothered to remove his shoes, is getting the full benefit. London's second busiest railway terminus (after Waterloo), Victoria Station opened in 1860, originally as two stations, one built by the London, Brighton and South Coast Railway, the other by the South Eastern & Chatham Railway; they merged in 1924. Famous express trains the *Golden Arrow*, *Brighton Belle* and *Night Ferry* once departed from its platforms, and fans of Oscar Wilde will know that the hero of *The Importance of Being Earnest* was found in a handbag in the station's cloakroom.

Keystone/Hulton Archive

Carry On tea break 1971

Everyone's favourite Cockney was in reality, of course, a mockney; South African-born Sid James arrived in England on Christmas Day 1946 and within a decade had launched a brilliant TV and film career as a chirpy Cockney, which worked as a great foil to Tony Hancock's more lugubrious character in *Hancock's Half Hour*, on which James met Kenneth Williams. Here the two stars take a tea break (with Patsy Rowlands on the right) during the filming of *Carry On at Your Convenience*; despite a long working relationship the pair weren't close, and Sid was openly uncomfortable with Ken's overt homosexuality. Shot at and around Pinewood, and in Brighton, the film would prove to be the least successful of the 31 Carry On films, its spoofing of trade unions alienating its largely working-class fan base.

Larry Ellis Collection/Hulton Archive

Southall cinema 1976

Nowadays, Bollywood is big news in London, with numerous filmmakers choosing to shoot here and plenty of cinemas specialising in screening the results. But back in 1976 it was only possible to see Indian films on the big screen in a few locations, such as west London's Southall, which has been home to one of the capital's largest Indian communities since the '50s. While the influx of immigrants into the area (most recently, Somalis fleeing their country's civil war) is often associated with its proximity to Heathrow Airport, immigration started long before the airport opened in 1946; as far back as the 1920s Southall saw many economic migrants escaping the poverty and terrible working conditions much closer to home, in Wales.

Central Press/Hulton Archive

Pub in Dulwich 1905

A night down the pub in Dulwich at the turn of the 20th century seems to have been a grim affair: bare floor, hard bench seating, dim lighting and only a few adverts for decoration. The male-only clientele doesn't exactly look like a barrel of laughs either. But then this would have been the public bar, a no-frills space designed for working men to slake their thirst with cheap beer. The distinctive red triangle logo for Bass Pale Ale – visible in no less than three framed pictures on the walls, and still in use today – was Britain's first registered trademark; company lore has it that an employee waited overnight at the patent office to be at the front of the queue on 1 January 1876, the day the Trademark Registration Act came into force.
Reinhold Thiele/Hulton Archive

Notting Hill fashion 1967

The shop that launched a thousand looks in Swinging London, I Was Lord Kitchener's Valet started life in 1964 as a Portobello Road stall selling retro military threads and other Empire ephemera. Three years later, the word had spread: Hendrix had purchased his iconic braided uniform jacket, Eric Clapton and the Who had popped in, the shop had provided inspiration for Peter Blake's album cover for *Sgt Pepper*, and two more outlets – on the King's Road and Carnaby Street – had opened. Robert Orbach, one of the shops' directors, recalled: 'I'm sitting there one morning and in walked John Lennon, Mick Jagger and Cynthia Lennon. And I didn't know whether I was hallucinating… Jagger bought a red Grenadier Guards drummer's jacket, probably for about £5. The next morning there was a line of 100 people wanting to buy this tunic… and we sold everything in the shop by lunchtime.'

Popperfoto

Lord Kitchener 1956

Aldwyn 'Lord Kitchener' Roberts was already a huge calypso star in Trinidad by the time he boarded the *Empire Windrush* for London in 1948. For the 500 other West Indian immigrants on the ship, and the thousands who would follow, he became the embodiment of home, the strong narratives and catchy melodies of his compositions reminding them of the life they'd left behind. By the time this photo was taken, his witty, bawdy, part-poetry, part-reportage songs were delighting black and white audiences alike, but most popular were the bittersweet tunes that spoke of the migrant's thwarted hopes, loneliness and longing to return home. In 1962 Kitch did just that, picking up a career in Trinidad that saw him win the prestigious carnival road march competition a record-breaking ten times between 1965 and 1976.

Popperfoto

Reading a comic 1968

While dad admires the displays at the Royal Horticultural Society flower and vegetable show in Victoria, his two young sons pore over the latest edition of the *Hotspur* weekly comic. The *Hotspur* first appeared in 1933 as a story paper (containing such thrilling tales as Buffalo Bill's Schooldays, The Truant Catcher and Japers of the Red Circle, the first of a constant stream of stories about Red Circle School), turning to the strip cartoon format in 1959. Produced by Dundee-based publishing giant DC Thomson, it was one of Britain's most popular comics, though never matched the readership of the *Eagle* or the longevity of DC's the *Beano* (established 1938) and the *Dandy* (1937), both of which survive today. After a series of mergers with other titles, the *Hotspur* folded in 1981.

Homer Sykes

David Low 1938

Britain's most famous political cartoonist of the 20th century concentrates on his latest creation for the *Evening Standard*. A New Zealander by birth, Low came to London in 1919 to work for left-wing newspaper the *Star*. He also contributed to *Punch*, the *New Statesman*, *Daily Herald*, *Manchester Guardian* and *Picture Post*, but he's best known for his wartime cartoons for the *Standard*. He joined the paper in 1927 – having won a guarantee of editorial independence from owner Lord Beaverbrook – and remained until 1950, drawing up to four cartoons a week. His merciless attacks on Hitler and Mussolini made him loathed in Germany and Italy, while his most famous character, the pompous, buffoonish, pig-headed Colonel Blimp (who first appeared in 1934), enraged the British establishment. Low always worked from his Hampstead home, advising 'You don't want to get too friendly with editors. Gives them ideas above their station.'

The Kinks 1966

North London band the Kinks (left to right, Peter Quaife, brothers Ray and Dave Davies, and Mick Avory) pose cryptically on a cannon in front of Tower Bridge at the height of their fame in the mid 1960s. Their brand of hard-driving rock and satirical, observational lyrics is now seen as one of the most influential (and notably English) sounds of the late 20th century. This picture was taken at a difficult time for the band, however. Ray Davies, front man and songwriter, suffered a nervous breakdown, and other personal and legal problems were to beset the group. Still, the following year produced some of their best songs, including 'Sunny Afternoon', 'Waterloo Sunset', 'Autumn Almanac' and 'Dead End Street'.
Reprise Records/Warner Bros/Hulton Archive

Lost property office 1929

Londoners have always been a forgetful lot – if this pre-war photo of the lost property office at Waterloo Station is anything to go by. Nowadays, Transport for London's lost property office at Baker Street handles around 170,000 misplaced items a year, abandoned on tubes, trains, buses, trams and taxis, including about 16,000 umbrellas – as well as false teeth, bones, stuffed animals and the occasional breast implant. The long-suffering staff field about 800 calls a day from absent-minded passengers, and a computer programme (called, aptly enough, 'Sherlock') is used to match object with owner. After three months, unclaimed items are either donated to charities such as the Salvation Army or sold at auction.
Fox Photos/Hulton Archive

Lord Leighton 1885

Painter, sculptor, cosmopolitan traveller, President of the Royal Academy and all-round eminent Victorian, Frederic, Lord Leighton sits in the first-floor studio of his home in Holland Park, surrounded by his work. The studio, and the rest of the house – including the spectacular Arab Hall with its walls covered in Syrian tiles – is now a museum, Leighton House, and a popular spot for wedding receptions. Assorted paintings, sculptures and drawings by Leighton are on display at the house, as well as at Tate Britain, the National Gallery and the V&A. Unfortunately, his most famous and iconic work, *Flaming June*, isn't in London. It was found languishing in a shop in Amsterdam in the 1960s, and purchased by the owner of the Ponce Museum of Art in Puerto Rico, where it still resides.

Mayall/Hulton Archive

Petticoat Lane Market 1951

Shoppers are reflected in an array of mirrors at Sunday's Petticoat Lane Market in the East End. Petticoat Lane itself doesn't exist; the thoroughfare became Middlesex Street in 1830, though the old name (originally Peticote) persists. It's one of London's oldest and most traditional markets; clothes and bric-a-brac – still a mainstay, alongside household goods, leather goods and electronics – have been sold here since the turn of the 17th century, and successive waves of immigration ensured the area was long the centre of the city's garment trade. Sunday trading is a result of the preponderance of Jewish stallholders, who couldn't work on the sabbath. Competition from gentrified Spitalfields Market and Brick Lane hasn't dampened its popularity; it's still hard to move through the punters browsing the 1,000-plus stalls (Alan Sugar was one of many entrepreneurs who got his start here).
Ernst Haas

Workers at Dagenham 1933

Known as the 'Detroit of Europe', Ford's vast motor factory at Dagenham cost the American company a fortune to build in 1931 and at its peak was Europe's largest car-manufacturing plant, employing more than 40,000 people, with its own power station and foundry. Just two years after opening, the workforce mobilised for the first time (as this photo shows) against wage cuts. It would be the first of many disputes at the plant, where trade unions and management clashed for decades – memorably in the late 1960s over the fact that female machinists were paid less than men who swept floors, a cause taken up by employment secretary Barbara Castle, leading to the 1970 Equal Pay Act. A series of much-loved cars, from the Zephyr to the Escort and the Capri, rolled off Dagenham's assembly lines, but production came to an end in 2000.

Topical Press Agency/Hulton Archive

The Sex Pistols 1977

An iconic moment in the short sharp history of punk as London upstarts the Sex Pistols, with new member Sid Vicious (in the centre, pointing) and band manager and Sex boutique owner Malcolm McLaren (to his right), sign a new contract with A&M Records outside Buckingham Palace on 10 March. The contract was terminated after only six days, to be picked up two months later by Virgin Records. From three labels in less than six months, the canny McLaren had milked the national brouhaha over the band's expletives-filled interview on ITV's early evening show *Today* for all it was worth. Anarchy in the UK ensued, with cancelled gigs and protests assuring the band's notoriety and spurring a powerful new musical and cultural movement.

Graham Wood/Evening Standard/Hulton Archive

Henry Cooper
1958

'Our 'Enery', the Catford boy who found fame in the boxing ring, sports an impressive shiner the day after outpointing Zora Folley over ten rounds at Wembley. Britain's most famous, and most popular, boxer for several decades, Cooper was renowned for his left hook, known as ''Enery's 'ammer'. He was British, European and Commonwealth heavyweight champion in 1970, but is probably best remembered for felling Cassius Clay (later Muhammad Ali) at Wembley in 1963 – and, post-retirement, for encouraging the public to 'splash it all over' as the face of Brut aftershave. He unveiled his own blue plaque, at the gym where he trained above the Thomas a Becket Pub in the Old Kent Road, in 2008, 50 years after the Folley fight.

Edward Miller/Keystone/Hulton Archive

Laurence Olivier and Noël Coward
1930

Noël Coward's comedy of manners *Private Lives* brought Britain's best-known writer together with the actor who would come to be considered by many as the 20th-century's finest. Laurence Olivier, seen here (left) preparing for a fight scene with Coward at the Phoenix Theatre, was on the verge of stardom, with Coward's comedy of manners his stage breakthrough at the age of 23. The production was a hit both in London and on Broadway. Olivier's acting career spanned six decades; in 1963 he became the first artistic director of the National Theatre. Coward (born in Teddington) had an equally long and acclaimed working life and was nicknamed 'the Master' for managing to combine multiple roles – playwright, actor, composer, singer, director and fashionable man about town – with effortless wit and sophistication. Olivier read at his memorial service in St Martin's-in-the-Fields in 1973.

Sasha/Hulton Archive

Bertrand Russell 1961

At the grand old age of 88, mathematician, philosopher and pacificist Bertrand Russell addresses the crowd at a CND rally in Trafalgar Square. Seven months later, he was arrested and threatened with imprisonment for organising a sit-down protest in Whitehall. Born into the aristocracy, Russell succeeded to the title 3rd Earl Russell but refused to use it. His brilliance won him the Nobel prize for literature in 1950, but his interest in politics earned him wider recognition outside intellectual circles. In 1918 he was sent to Brixton Prison for six months following an arrest for 'vehement conduct in the cause of pacifism'. A blue plaque at 34 Russell Chambers, Bury Place, WC1 pinpoints his Bloomsbury home.
Cleland Rimmer/Hulton Archive

Kensington Gardens 1922

Generations of London children have sailed their toy boats on the Round Pond in Kensington Gardens. More of a squashed square than a circle, the pond was created when the gardens were redesigned in the 18th century, as the private grounds of Kensington Palace, the home of Queen Caroline, wife of George II. The Model Yacht Sailing Association (MYSA), the oldest such club in the country, has been using the pond since 1876, though nowadays radio-controlled vessels have supplanted wind-powered models. The pond is in some ways too big to be used as a boating lake, and yachts often got becalmed in the centre if the wind dropped. When the water was drained in 1923, the remains of 150 yachts were found stuck in the mud at the bottom.

Topical Press Agency/Hulton Archive

Sightseeing bus 1907

Tourist trips around the capital by open-topped bus are not a modern phenomenon – as is clear from this photo of a smart new motor charabanc setting out from Paddington Station on a London sightseeing trip. The tours were run by bus company Motor Jobmasters in conjunction with Great Western Railway, scooping up passengers as they disgorged from the terminus for trains from the West Country. Improved rail connections at the end of the 19th century ushered in a whole new era of day-tripping to the capital, and the new petrol-powered buses – introduced in 1904 by Thomas Tilling on his company's Peckham to Oxford Circus route – were ready and waiting to transport them around the city.

Hulton Archive

Rita Webb and Sidney Poitier 1966

Willesden girl Rita Webb was probably more at home in the East End's Watney Market than elegant Hollywood superstar Sidney Poitier. The pair are filming Poitier's English-made blockbuster, *To Sir, with Love* (based on the novel by ER Braithwaite), in which he starred as an idealistic teacher in a tough-nut east London school; red-haired Webb played feisty parent Mrs Joseph. Already an Oscar winner by this point, Poitier eventually turned his hand to directing and a globetrotting role as an ambassador for the Bahamas. After an early career in music hall, Webb settled to frequent – if not starring – roles as a cockney harridan, becoming a half-familiar figure in television comedies. She was happy to remain in London, living for 40 years in Chepstow Road, Bayswater.

Harry Todd/Hulton Archive

Alfred Hitchcock 1955

Celebrated *Picture Post* photographer Thurston Hopkins took this enigmatic shot of Alfred Hitchcock outside the British Museum in January 1955 for an article entitled 'A Sinister Time Was Had By All', in which the filmmaker and Leytonstone-born son of a poulterer revealed his fascination with ambiguous half shadows. By this time Hitch had been in Hollywood for 16 years, where he had already made many of his most famous films, including *Spellbound* (1945), *Notorious* (1946) and *Rear Window* (1954). His trips to London were infrequent (though he did shoot *Frenzy* in the capital in 1972); on this occasion, he was en route to St Moritz with his wife and life-long professional collaborator Alma Reville, a romantic return to the site of their honeymoon in 1926.

Thurston Hopkins/Picture Post/Hulton Archive

George Melly 1960

Self-titled 'Goodtime George' Melly plays, as he did for more than a decade, with Mick Mulligan's Magnolia jazz band in a London club. In a cultural life that spanned almost 60 years, the joyously decadent Melly performed hundreds of gigs as a jazz and blues singer, usually in his trademark striped zoot suit and fedora, but he was also a lauded critic, writer and lecturer on subjects as diverse as music, film, TV and art history, in particular surrealism and Pop art. In print as on stage, the lewd, crude and sexually adventurous tales of this cultural explorer endeared him to readers of such varied publications as *Punch*, the *Observer* and the *Daily Mail*. Melly even refused to be cowed by the onset of lung cancer and dementia in later life, saying that 'as a surrealist, I quite enjoy having dementia'. He died in 2007 at the age of 80, a month after a final (and suitably bizarre) gig at Oxford Street's 100 Club.

Ray Moreton/Keystone/Hulton Archive

Windmill dancers 1940

While much of recreational life in London was necessarily curtailed during World War II, some entertainments continued undaunted, offering respite from the horrors and helping maintain morale. Soho's Windmill Theatre famously stayed open throughout – with the exception of the compulsory 12-day shutdown during the Blitz – resulting in its well-known motto, 'we never closed'. The theatre's *Revudeville* tableaux performers and dancers would even practise their routines wearing gas masks and hard hats when necessary. (The National Gallery, which sent its collection to the countryside for safekeeping, also provided unbroken wartime entertainment – albeit of a very different kind. Classical pianist Myra Hess, concerned about the capital's lack of culture, held weekly lunchtime concerts there that ran without interruption from 1939 to 1946.)
Hulton Archive

Cat-meat sellers 1909

Cat-meat men and women like these indomitable figures in Camberwell were once a common sight on London's streets. Fortunately for the city's moggies, 'cat's meat' consisted of skewers of beef or horsemeat, which were sold to cat owners before the invention of processed pet food. Which isn't to say that cats weren't eaten by less-discerning (or less well-off) Londoners; meat from a cat, known as cat flesh, was sometimes consumed, particularly during rationing in World War II, when a surfeit of stray cats fattened on the excess numbers of vermin in London's bombed-out buildings would occasionally find their way into 'rabbit' stews and pies.

Hulton Archive

Einstein and Shaw 1930

German-born physicist and Nobel Prize winner Albert Einstein and Irish playwright George Bernard Shaw attend a dinner at the Savoy hotel on 28 October 1930. In the centre, and looking like Shaw's long-lost twin, is their host, Baron Lionel Walter Rothschild – banker, politician and keen zoologist – who had organised the event as a fund-raiser for the tide of eastern European Jewish refugees sweeping westward. As master of ceremonies, Shaw, an old friend of Einstein's (the two had met nine years earlier at a dinner party in London), was unabashed in his fulsome praise of the guest of honour, famously describing him as a 'maker of universes'.

Topical Press Agency/Hulton Archive

Lew Grade 1978

One of London's great showbiz impresarios was born Lev Winogradsky in the Ukraine in 1906. His family fled the Russian pogroms in 1912 and settled in the East End. He started out in the rag trade, became a professional dancer, then a talent agent and, in the 1950s, formed his own television company (later ATV), producing iconic shows such as *The Saint*, *The Prisoner*, *Stingray* and *Thunderbirds*. But his biggest coup was Jim Henson's *Muppet Show*. Initially rejected by the big US networks, the show was shot at the ATV studios in Borehamwood between 1976 and 1981. It became a smash hit. Here, Grade meets Fozzie Bear at a Variety Club awards lunch at the Savoy hotel. Henson immortalised Grade (who died in 1998) in the form of the Muppet scientist, Dr Bunsen Honeydew.

Malcolm Clarke/Keystone/Hulton Archive

Dan Leno
1896

Born George Galvin in 1860 in Somers Town, Dan Leno made his debut at Paddington's Cosmotheca Music Hall as 'Little George, the Infant Wonder, Contortionist and Posturer'. He remained little – only reaching five foot three inches – but developed a successful stage act around Cockney humour, pantomime (always playing the dame) and clog-dancing. Here he plays the Baroness in *Cinderella* at Drury Lane. He topped many theatre bills, often playing opposite Marie Lloyd and even entertaining Edward VII at Sandringham. Thousands mourned his tragically early death at the age of 43; *The Times* wrote 'to find anything like a close parallel to his style, we should probably have to go back to the Italian commedia dell'arte'. He is buried in Lambeth Cemetery under the inscription 'Here sleeps the King of Laughter-Makers'.

Hulton Archive

Lottie Collins
1880

Another Victorian music hall star, East Ender
Charlotte Louisa ('Lottie') Collins started in
showbiz as a skipping rope dancer at the
tender age of ten. She went on to become
a vaudeville actress and while touring the
States as the 'Originator of Skirt Dancing'
first heard the song 'Ta-ra-ra, boom-de-ay!'
She obtained the English rights and it soon
became her signature tune, along with the
risqué high kicks that punctuated each
'boom', exposing her garters and bare thighs.
(A century later, her garters were sold at
Sotheby's.) Poor health – a heart condition
thought to be exacerbated by her energetic
dance routines – led to an early death at
the age of 44. She is buried in Islington
and St Pancras Cemetery in East Finchley.
London Stereoscopic Company

Surrealist exhibition 1936

Although French writer and poet André Breton published the Surrealist Manifesto in 1924 and his group of artistic disciples held their first exhibition in Paris a year later, it took more than a decade for the movement to cross the Channel. This photo marks the occasion of London's first International Surrealist Exhibition, which was held in June 1936 at the New Burlington Galleries, and featured, among others, heavyweight Salvador Dalí (back row, third from left). Painter Roland Penrose and critic Herbert Read (back row, fifth and sixth from left) formed the selection committee, picking many works by their European counterparts. The show provoked a hostile public reaction, with Surrealism in Britain branded as foreign rubbish. But the exhibition made an impact on young British artists; Henry Moore and Paul Nash were two notable supporters.

Evening Standard/Hulton Archive

Wandsworth brewery 1946

Young's worker Ronnie Fordham endures his 'trussing in' ceremony at the firm's Ram Brewery in Wandsworth. The ceremony was traditional to brew houses across the country and marked the transition from apprentice to fully-fledged cooper. The recipient was first covered in a tar-like substance by his workmates, then put in a barrel and 'feathered' with wood shavings (as pictured here). Only after being 'baptised' by a pint over the head, would he finally be presented with a key to signify the end of his seven-year apprenticeship – along with a pint (or several) of bitter to celebrate. A commercial brewery was first recorded on Young's Wandsworth site in 1581, which made the Ram London's oldest – until 2006, when the last barrels left the brewery and it closed for good.

Bert Hardy/Picture Post/Hulton Archive

The Beach Boys 1964

On a typically grey day in London the phenomenally successful Beach Boys pose cheesily for the camera. Three years earlier, the three Wilson brothers from Hawthorne, California, their cousin and a school friend had formed a pop group whose joyous harmonies and invocations of suntans and surfing struck gold in their own country. This, their first trip to London, saw them broadcasting their melodious brand of musical sunshine from a studio in the EMI building on Manchester Square, as well as radio shows for the BBC. Their hard work was rewarded when, in 1966, the Beach Boys were voted number one group in the world by the UK music press, leaving their main rivals, the Beatles, in their wake.
Michael Ochs Archives

Serpentine swimmers 1935

Despite the capital's less than balmy climate, Londoners have always embraced outdoor bathing. The city once had more than 50 open-air swimming pools; the Serpentine Lido in Hyde Park is still hugely popular, though only members of the Serpentine Swimming Club (established 1864) brave its icy waters in winter, culminating in the famous Peter Pan race on Christmas Day – when the water temperature can drop to below 40°F (4°C). The South London Swimming Club, based at Tooting Bec Lido, is almost as venerable, having been founded in 1906. It also holds races on Christmas Day, Boxing Day and New Year's Day and inaugurated the first UK Cold Water Swimming Championships in 2006.

JA Hampton/Hulton Archive

Anthony Blunt 1962

Looking typically aloof and patrician, Sir Anthony Blunt poses in front of a Velázquez in 1962 – just a couple of years before he confessed to being the 'Fourth Man' in the Cambridge spy network of Guy Burgess, Donald Maclean and Kim Philby. But his treasonable past was officially kept secret until he was outed by Margaret Thatcher in 1979. Public outrage was fuelled by the fact that he'd been allowed to become such a respected establishment figure – a wartime member of MI5, he was an eminent art critic and historian and served as both director of the Courtauld Institute and Surveyor of the Queen's Pictures for almost 30 years. He died in 1983, publicly disgraced, humiliated and stripped of his knighthood (awarded in 1956). His unfinished memoirs, currently in the British Library, are due for release in 2013.

Lee/Hulton Archive

Cilla, Petula and Sandie
1965

Pop stars Cilla Black, Petula Clark and Sandie Shaw (from left to right) look chummy at the Dorchester Hotel for a Variety Club luncheon. The three young stars epitomised the spirit of pop in 1960s Britain, though perhaps Sandie Shaw, with her barefoot performances, best captured the emerging hippy era. Occasional attempts to escape her image were put paid to in 1967 when she was chosen to represent Britain in the Eurovision Song Contest. Her entry, 'Puppet on a String', won the contest easily, and Shaw was doomed to keep churning out pop singles despite the more thoughtful, alternative material on her albums. She did eventually acquire an indie career that saw her cover the Smiths' song 'Hand In Glove,' while long-time fans Johnny Marr and Morrissey were inspired by her song 'Heaven Knows I'm Missing Him Now' to write their own version.

Fred Mott/Hulton Archive

Private Eye 1963

The co-founders of satirical magazine *Private Eye* (from left to right, editors Richard Ingrams and Christopher Booker, and cartoonist Willie Rushton) keep up the good work as the publication faces its first libel suit. Randolph Churchill, son of Winston, was the first in a long, illustrious and ever-increasing line of litigants who have taken on the magazine since it first went to press in 1961. He objected to a cartoon that portrayed him as a boozy old soak dubbed 'Rudolph Rednose', who needed help writing a biography of his famous father. As has been the case on numerous instances subsequently, *Private Eye* eventually agreed to pay damages (£3,000) and to print an apology in the *Evening Standard*. The magazine has long been based in Soho, first at Greek Street and, currently, at Carlisle Street.

John Pratt/Keystone/Hulton Archive

Brick Lane silk weaver 1930

Silk weaver Mary White was the last of a dying breed in 1930, when she was visited by Mrs Stanley Baldwin (wife of the former prime minister) and assorted hangers-on. Around 50,000 Huguenots had arrived in east London in the 17th century, fleeing religious persecution in Catholic France. With their Protestant work ethic, skills and solidarity, they soon transformed Spitalfields into 'Weaver Town'; many of the immigrants were silk weavers from Lyon, who used a new technique that gave the material a glossy finish and fuelled a fashion trend among London's upper classes. Mechanisation in the 19th century spelled the end for the Spitalfields hand-weavers, though their legacy lives on in the area's distinctive architecture and place names such as Fournier Street, Nantes Place, Fashion Street and Silk Street.

Popperfoto

Herbert Morrison 1941

Clementine Churchill, the aristocratic, Mayfair-born prime minister's wife, and Lambeth lad Herbert Morrison, recently appointed home secretary, bond over his namesake: a self-assembly indoor air-raid shelter designed to squash by no more than 12 inches if a house collapsed. The protective cage was the invention of structural engineer John Fleetwood Baker, and half a million were distributed by the end of 1941. This demonstration, entitled 'Safety from Bombing', took place as London was still reeling from the Blitz. The death and destruction in the East End had a major impact on Morrison, a former mayor of Hackney and ex-leader of the London County Council.

Popperfoto

Spitalfields Market 1928

The fruit and vegetable market seen here in May 1928 is a far cry from the tourist magnet that Spitalfields has become since the wholesale fruit and veg traders were moved to New Spitalfields Market, Leyton, in 1991. A market had operated in and around the east London site for centuries, but in 1684 construction began on a formal building (though it wasn't covered until the late 19th century); in 1920 the City of London took charge of the market, extending the original buildings eight years later. Second only to Covent Garden Market in size and importance, Spitalfields operated through the night, with traders such as M Israel selling to greengrocers, restaurateurs and hoteliers.

SR Gaiger/Topical Press Agency/Hulton Archive

William Booth 1900

Now a worldwide church with more than one and half million members, the Salvation Army started out as a humble East End mission, mixing evangelising with good works among the poor and destitute. Founded by William Booth and his wife Catherine in 1865, the organisation initially met with hostility from the Church and the authorities. It was renamed the Salvation Army in 1878, adopting military-style uniforms and ranks, and soon became famous for its soup kitchens and hostels, as well as its streetside services accompanied by much waving of banners, banging of drums and shaking of tambourines. Booth is seen here with his eldest son and successor, William Bramwell Booth (perched awkwardly atop the table – possibly because, by this time, his father was almost blind). William Senior died in 1912, aged 83, and is buried, as were most Victorian non-conformists, in Abney Park Cemetery in Stoke Newington.

London Stereoscopic Company/Hulton Archive

Bob and Paula 1985

Looking uncharacteristically beatific backstage at Wembley Stadium during Live Aid (13 July 1985), Bob Geldof takes a break with his partner Paula Yates from 16 hours of urging an estimated audience of 1.5 billion in 100 countries to 'Give us the money NOW.' The concert, a fundraiser for famine relief in Ethiopia, involved massive live concerts in London and Philadelphia and smaller events around the globe. It would eventually raise £150m, but seven hours into the concert, the total of £1.2m was disappointing enough to invoke Geldof's famous exhortation and a later outburst that deployed the word 'fuck' and caused donations to rise to £300 per second. Writer and TV presenter Yates would go on to divorce Geldof and take up with INXS frontman Michael Hutchence – a tragic union that culminated in his suicide in 1997, and her death by accidental overdose in 2000.

Dave Hogan/Hulton Archive

Daniel Farson 1952

A typical summer scene is captured by celebrated photographer, writer, broadcaster and Soho character Dan Farson in 1952, when a heatwave saw thousands of Londoners flock to the capital's parks to sunbathe (or cool off). Farson was fascinated by class issues in Britain and the changing face of a nation in transition (the photos were commissioned by *Picture Post*, but never published). Despite – or perhaps because of – being an alcoholic misfit who always saw himself as an outsider, Farson's poignant photos, excellent newspaper features and cutting-edge documentary TV series for new channel ITV covered myriad topics, including nudism, teenagers, poverty, illiteracy, accents, sex education and even witchcraft – the latter a fitting subject for the great-nephew of *Dracula* author Bram Stoker.
Daniel Farson/Picture Post/Hulton Archive

Mitford sisters 1932

This snap of three of the six Mitford sisters – Unity, Diana and Nancy (from left to right) – at a society wedding in March 1932 shows them in typically haughty pose. All three were born in London but soon after this picture was taken would follow very different paths across Europe, Nancy becoming a celebrated author, Unity and Diana travelling to Germany first in 1932 as admirers of Adolf Hitler, then as part of the British delegation to the 1933 Nuremberg Rally, where Unity would meet and befriend the dictator. Just a month before this photo, noted beauty Diana had met Oswald Mosley, with whom she embarked on a four-year public affair before marrying him at the house of Joseph Goebbels in 1936. Hitler, the only guest, gave the couple a silver-framed picture of himself as a wedding gift.

Hulton Archive

Finsbury Park squat 1976

Squatting was big news in London in the 1970s and early '80s, when an increasing number of people, for political, economic or lifestyle reasons, took over empty or abandoned properties – such as these council houses in Charteris Road, N4. Squatting polarised views across communities, some seeing the action as a valid political and pragmatic response to the shortage of public housing, others resentful of what they saw as freeloading shirkers trashing the neighbourhood and angering local residents with anti-social behaviour. In 1979 there were thought to be 30,000 squatters in the capital; today the Advisory Service for Squatters estimates there are just over half that number.

Evening Standard/Hulton Archive

Milkmen in Maida Vale 1931

As far back as the early 1930s people were having groceries delivered to their homes along with their milk, as this shot of United Dairies employees in north London shows. Domestic milk delivery had come a long way by this point: herds of cows were still kept in London until the 1870s, when Express Dairies began transporting milk supplies by rail from countryside depots. A decade later, Express pioneered the use of the milk bottle (before its invention customers' jugs would be filled straight from the churn), which came in multiple sizes until after World War II, when the one-pint bottle took over. Pasteurisation was standard by the end of the 19th century, but the horse-drawn cart didn't disappear until the electric milk float became widespread in the '50s.

Topical Press Agency/Hulton Archive

Linton Kwesi Johnson
1984

Influential reggae dub poet Linton Kwesi Johnson, with trademark hat and goatee, performs at the Lyceum. The Jamaican-born writer, hailed 'the alternative poet laureate' by *Time Out* magazine, came to south London when he was 12. While still at Tulse Hill secondary school he organised poetry workshops with the Black Panthers. He came to prominence as a poet and musician during Margaret Thatcher's premiership, the era of the Notting Hill and Brixton riots, when race relations were at an all-time low in Britain. His first volume of poetry, *Voices of the Living and the Dead*, was published in 1974, followed swiftly by his three best-known albums, *Dread Beat an' Blood*, *Forces of Victory* and *Bass Culture*. He is the first black (and second living) poet to have his work published in Penguin's Modern Classics series.

David Corio/Redferns

Charles Dickens
1860

A keen eye for the evils and injustices of Victorian London, a sharp ear for dialogue, a benign wit and a work ethic instilled at a young age earned novelist Charles Dickens superstar status on both sides of the Atlantic. Today his style might be considered as florid as his dress sense, but his books have never gone out of print, and televisual adaptations of his stories attract record-breaking viewing figures. He never stopped working – the drive to make money was undoubtedly linked to seeing his father in Marshalsea debtors' prison in Borough – and his gruelling tour schedule undoubtedly shortened his life. He insisted that no memorial should be erected to him, but his remains lie in Poets' Corner in Westminster Abbey and his Doughty Street home has become a museum.

London Stereoscopic Company/Hulton Archive

Haile Selassie 1936

The 1930s were a mixed decade for the emperor of Abyssinia, Haile Selassie ('Power of the Trinity'), seen here with daughter Tshai and son Asfa Wossen. Six years after being crowned emperor of Ethiopia, Ras Tafari Makonnen was forced to flee the country, his empire crushed by Benito Mussolini's invasion of Ethiopia. He went to London and then to Malvern. It was a sad, low point for the man regarded by Rastafarians as the physical presence of God (Jah) on earth and the first black person to appear on the cover of *Time* magazine in 1930. Things could have been worse; in fleeing his homeland Selassie managed to take 42 crates of belongings, and was housed in a sumptuous house overlooking Hyde Park.

New York Times Co/Hulton Archive

Hippies crossing a road 1967

Four trendily dressed hipsters draw curious glances from passers-by in a London street in 1967. That year brought the 'Summer of Love', and was when the counterculture crossed over into the mainstream. Scott McKenzie's song 'San Francisco' became a hit in Europe as well as the States, and hippy clothing was just as likely to be worn as a fashion statement as it was as a declaration of alternative philosophy or politics. In the capital, popular underground clubs were UFO on Tottenham Court Road and Middle Earth in Covent Garden; happening boutiques included Granny Takes a Trip, on the King's Road; and in February 1967 the first edition of *Oz* magazine appeared.

Archive Photos/Hulton Archive

Spanish Civil War mural 1939

British support for the left-wing Republicans fighting Franco and fascism during the Spanish Civil War was widespread; more than 2,000 Britons went to fight, document or do what they could, others dedicated themselves to raising money and providing relief action at home. Artists, mobilised by the Artists International Association, played a key role in this support; Felicia Browne and George Orwell went to Spain to record and express the horrors, others (as here) painted street hoardings and murals to raise funds. Picasso's *Guernica*, created in response to the bombing of the Basque village in 1937, went on international tour; Surrealist artist Roland Penrose arranged for its two-week showing at the Whitechapel Gallery in January 1939, where it was seen by 12,000 visitors on the first day. Admission was the price of a pair of boots (as decreed by Picasso), which were then sent to the Spanish front.

John F Stephenson/Topical Press Agency/Hulton Archive

Arsenal fans 1972

1972 was the year Arsenal fans, known as Gunners (or, in the more recent vernacular, Gooners), fervently hoped that their team would replicate their FA Cup success of the previous year, when they won the FA Cup and League double. Arsenal had already relinquished their league title to the charismatic Brian Clough's Derby County and been knocked out of the European Cup by the eventual winners Ajax. To win the FA Cup in consecutive seasons would be a feat rarely managed and would match the achievement of Arsenal's north London arch rivals, Tottenham Hotspur, a decade earlier. In the event, Arsenal lost 1-0 to a better Leeds side captained by Billy Bremner and featuring Leeds legends Jack Charlton, Norman 'Bite Yer Legs' Hunter, Johnny Giles and Allan Clarke.

Geroge W Hales/Hulton Archive

Marsha Rowe and Rosie Boycott
1972

Young editors Rosie Boycott (standing) and Marsha Rowe prepare to launch a new magazine for women, *Spare Rib*. The first issue of this determinedly unglossy publication sold out, despite several newsagents, including WH Smith, refusing to stock it. A passionate feminist response to the values traditionally espoused by women's magazines, *Spare Rib* proved a valuable launch pad for the careers of both women, who went on to set up Virago Press with Carmen Callil. Rowe then developed her career in book publishing and Boycott became a successful editor of national newspapers after, amusingly, doubling the circulation of men's magazine *Esquire*, just as *Spare Rib* was coming to the end of the line in 1993.
Sydney O'Meara/Evening Standard/Hulton Archive

Sylvia Pankhurst 1912

Sylvia Pankhurst embraced many causes – women's suffrage, socialism, pacifism, workers' rights, the independence of Ethiopia – in a long and busy life. Here she's painting the front of the Bow Road branch of the Women's Social & Political Union, the suffragette movement led by her mother Emmeline and sister Christabel; a few years later, she fell out with them over their support for World War I and their lack of interest in working-class rights. For 30 years she lived with (but never married) Italian anarchist Silvio Corio in Woodford on the edge of north-east London – Pankhurst Green opposite the tube station commemorates her link with the area. On Corio's death she emigrated to Ethiopia, where she was honoured with a state funeral in 1960.

John Thomson 1877

London cabbies have always had a mixed reputation, it seems. 'Despite the traditional hoarse voice, rough appearance and quarrelsome tone, cab-drivers are as a rule reliable and honest men' – so wrote Adolphe Smith in 1877; he provided the words to go with Scottish photographer John Thomson's picture of London cabmen (left), which appeared in the duo's pioneering publication, *Street Life in London*. One of the earliest examples of photography as social documentary, the book – which is still in print – also included buskers (below), chimney sweeps, fishmongers, ice-cream men, shoe-blacks, flower sellers and others who attempted to earn a living on the capital's streets. Lengthy interviews accompanied each photo, describing, often in harrowing detail, the hardships and privations facing London's poorest inhabitants.
John Thomson/Hulton Archive

Family in Shadwell 1920

Following World War I, London was in the grip of a serious slump that saw millions of families suffering through low wages, forced wage cuts or unemployment, despite the passing of the 1920 Unemployment Insurance Act, which extended unemployment benefit to cover most manual workers and lower-paid non-manual workers from the age of 16. Life in east London districts (such as Shadwell) in particular was harsh. For the unskilled labourer, days spent wandering the streets in search of work often led nowhere. Skilled dockers fared little better, the casual system of employment ensuring that most of them only worked two or three days a week. Consequently, subsistence levels of survival and meals of bread and nothing else were common.

Topical Press Agency/Hulton Archive

Robert Elms 1980

Hendon-born writer and broadcaster Robert Elms was an innocent-looking 20-year-old when this photo was taken, in the Blitz wine bar, the elitist nightspot on Covent Garden's Great Queen Street that witnessed the rapid rise and fall of the New Romantic movement. The 'Blitz Kids', including cloakroom attendant Boy George, doorman Steve Strange and bands such as Spandau Ballet and Visage, were known for their flamboyant and androgynous style – a direct reaction to the bleak austerity of the 1970s and the negativity of the punk genre. Elms (centre) was a key player and documentor of the scene, describing the Blitz as the 'club that heralded the 1980s'. His obsession with style has defined his reputation ever since; he went on to write for, and later edit, cult youth magazine *The Face*, and continues to write and broadcast today; he's had his own BBC London radio show since the '90s.

Homer Sykes/Premium Archive

Alan Bennett
1973

At the time of this protest in support of London's theatres in October 1973, Alan Bennett was already well known as a writer/performer (*Beyond the Fringe*) and playwright (*Forty Years On*), but it was still early in a career that would also encompass TV and radio dramas, films and best-selling memoirs. The Save London's Theatres Campaign (SLTC) was founded in 1972 by actors' union Equity, after the announcement of the GLC Covent Garden plan, which proposed the demolition of 12 West End theatres and the wrecking of another four. That campaign was successful, and the SLTC continues its work today, most recently in a bid to preserve Wilton's Music Hall in Whitechapel. Bennett lives in Camden, as he has done for more than 30 years.

Evening Standard/Hulton Archive

Bowling hoops in Hyde Park 1922

Ah, simpler times, when all a child needed for an afternoon's amusement was a warm coat and hat, stout shoes, a wooden hoop and stick – and a large park. 'Bowling', 'rolling' or 'trundling' hoops was especially popular in Victorian and Edwardian days, though it had been a favoured pastime since the days of ancient Greece and Rome, when adults as well as children used hoops as a form of exercise. By the time this photo was taken, there was competition from a host of new-fangled toys such as teddy bears (a German invention) and Meccano (British), though playtime staples like Monopoly (American) and Lego (Danish) didn't appear until the 1930s and '50s respectively.

Topical Press Agency/Hulton Archive

Equal rights demo 1968

Three female bus conductors at an Equal Pay for Equal Work demonstration in Trafalgar Square. Their placards demand the same rights as male bus conductors, as well as the same pay – though it wasn't until 1974 that London acquired its first female bus driver, Jill Viner, who drove the no.65. Protest covered many fronts in 1968; the equal pay struggle had been ignited by a strike at the Ford plant in Dagenham by women machinists who discovered that they were being paid less than men who swept the factory's floors. The strike gave rise to the National Joint Action Campaign for Women's Equal Rights, which resulted in the Equal Pay Act of 1970. Bus conductors, of both sexes, disappeared from London's streets, along with the iconic Routemaster, at the end of 2005.

Homer Sykes

Housing protest 1962

Protesters get their message across while heading to see housing minister Keith Joseph to demand the requisitioning of some of the capital's empty houses. Londoners faced a chronic housing shortage after World War II, with overcrowding and multiple-occupation being a particular problem in inner-city boroughs. Low-income families suffered most, and the 1957 Rent Act's removal of rent controls didn't help matters, adding 1,000 families to the homeless register each year. A massive council house building spree in the 1960s and '70s alleviated the problem somewhat, though the ill-judged design and shoddy construction of many of the new, usually high-rise estates meant that a third of the capital's local authority housing was deemed 'unfit' less than 30 years later.

Keystone/Hulton Archive

Cynthia Payne 1980

Bognor's jolliest daughter, Cynthia Payne, enjoys the attention bestowed on her in the year of her court hearing and imprisonment for keeping a disorderly house. The disorder in question was discovered in full swing when the police raided her home in Streatham during one of Ms Payne's popular sex parties. The entertainments, which involved exchanging luncheon vouchers for food, drink, striptease and some privacy with the girl of your choice, attracted streams of middle-aged and elderly gentlemen of good standing. In 1988 Cynthia Payne stood for parliament (unsuccessfully) with the Payne and Pleasure Party. She stayed in Streatham and went on to become a national treasure and frequent after-dinner speaker.

Evening Standard/Hulton Archive

Margaret Thatcher 1962

Conservative MP for Finchley Margaret Thatcher tries to show her human side on a ski run in Battersea Park. A year later the girl from Grantham would start her meteoric political rise with her appointment to pensions minister in Harold Macmillan's government; by the end of the decade a national love/hate relationship would begin with the slogan 'Thatcher, Thatcher, milk snatcher' when, as education secretary, she proposed to abolish free school milk. Elected prime minister on 4 May 1979, Thatcher led the country for 11 years until her resignation in 1990 on a wave of unpopularity brought about largely by her introduction of the poll tax. During that time she inspired veneration and enmity in equal measure, but when she famously labelled striking miners in 1984 as 'the enemy within' she became – and still is – universally loathed by Britain's left.

Reg Lancaster/Express/Hulton Archive

Oranges and lemons 1921

London's most famous nursery rhyme has long caused controversy over its reference to St Clement's, with ownership being contested by both St Clement Danes church on the Strand and St Clement Eastcheap in the City. While the latter, located near the one-time wharves where citrus fruit used to be unloaded, is more likely to have been the church alluded to in the counting rhyme, the lovely RAF church on the Strand does have one distinct claim on it, namely its ringing out of the rhyme's tune three times a day and an annual service after which the tune is played on hand bells, followed by the distribution of orange and lemons to pupils from the church's primary school – as pictured here.

Hulton Archive

Eduardo Paolozzi 1952

By the 1950s a new generation of sculptors was seeking recognition from a nation in love with Henry Moore. Eminent among them was Edinburgh-born Eduardo Paolozzi, whose career had been considerably enhanced by a commission to design a fountain for the 1951 Festival of Britain. 'Fish', the plaster model he's working on here, was included in the exhibition 15 Young Sculptors, at the Institute of Contemporary Arts (in its old home in Mayfair's Dover Street). As Pop art gained ground, Paolozzi was to describe himself as a pioneer of the movement. His work can be seen all over London, most notably in the form of a bronze of Isaac Newton outside the British Library, the large-scale 'Head of Invention' outside the Design Museum and the vivid mosaics in Tottenham Court Road tube station.

Edward G Malindine/Topical Press Agency/Hulton Archive

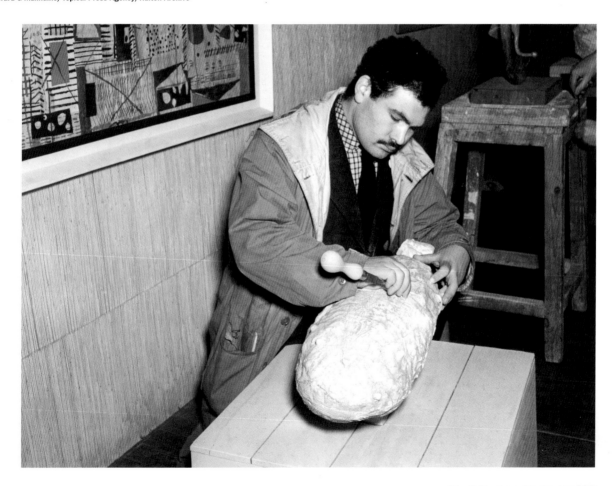

Radclyffe Hall 1927

Writer Radclyffe Hall, dressed in her trademark mannish clothes and short hair, with her long-time partner, Lady Una Troubridge, in their Kensington home; in the background is John Singer Sergeant's portrait of Hall's former lover, Mabel Batten. A year after this photograph was taken, Hall was embroiled in the furore surrounding the publication of her most famous book, *The Well of Loneliness*; the novel's favourable depiction of female homosexuality – or 'sexual inversion', in Hall's phrase – led to it being banned in Britain until after her death. This photo of Hall (heavily cropped to make her appear more masculine) was used by the *Sunday Express* in its campaign against the book. Hall died in 1943 and is buried in the grandiose Circle of Lebanon in Highgate Cemetery.

Fox Photos/Hulton Archive

World War I recruits 1914

A recruitment drive at Trafalgar Square in the first year of World War I, when the government was still relying on a system of voluntary enlistment (conscription was introduced in January 1916). Some of the earliest recruits were 'Pals' battalions: groups of friends or colleagues who joined and fought together. One of the first was the 10th (Service) Battalion of the Royal Fusiliers, the so-called Stockbrokers' Battalion; a recruiting office was set up on Throgmorton Street in the City in late August 1914, and within days 1,600 men had enlisted. Clapton Orient (now Leyton Orient) was the first English football league club to enlist as a group. Around 40 players and staff volunteered, and leading goal scorers Richard McFadden and William Jonas were among those killed in the Battle of the Somme.

Central Press/Hulton Archive

Danny Blanchflower
1954

He may look an unassuming chap, filing his studs in tie and buttoned cardigan, but Danny Blanchflower was one of the all-time great footballers, a master tactician and inspirational captain who led Tottenham Hotspur during its record-breaking season in 1961, when the team won the first 11 games of the season, drew the 12th and won the next four before going on to take the league championship (by eight points) and the FA Cup (beating Leicester City 2-0 in the final). He joined Spurs from Aston Villa, for the then enormous transfer fee of £30,000, and was also voted Player of the Year in 1958 and 1961. He always believed in football's emotional power, claiming: 'The game is about glory, it is about doing things in style and with a flourish, about going out and beating the other lot, not waiting for them to die of boredom.'

Keystone/Hulton Archive

John Gielgud
1930

The 1929/30 season at the Old Vic theatre was an auspicious one for 26-year-old John Gielgud (seen here checking his turban as he makes up for his role as Prospero): his performance as Hamlet, in the same season, was proclaimed by one critic to be the 'high-water mark of English Shakespearian acting of our time'. Born in South Kensington and educated at Westminster School and RADA, Gielgud had acting in his blood – he was the great-nephew of Victorian actress Dame Ellen Terry. Hamlet was the role that earned him universal adulation, but Prospero was the actor's favourite. Sixty years later, he was again feted for his interpretation of the magician – this time in Peter Greenaway's film *Prospero's Books*. Photographer Sasha (the professional name of Alexander Stewart) specialised in high society and theatrical portraits in the 1920s and '30s for the likes of *The Tatler* and *Illustrated London News*.
Sasha/Hulton Archive

Milk bar at Waterloo 1937

Customers down milky concoctions at a new portable milk bar that travelled between the platforms at Waterloo Station. It was the first of its kind at any station in Britain and the natural evolution of the static version, which had become increasingly popular in preceding years. Australian Hugh D McIntosh opened the first such enterprise in London in 1935 on Fleet Street; despite the hard-drinking hack clientele, the Black & White was a huge hit and milk bars soon spread throughout the country (Wales still has a number of National Milk Bars, the main rival to McIntosh's firm). An early forerunner of the plethora of coffee and juice shops that now crowd the capital's railway stations, the portable bars were especially popular during World War II with American troops.

Fox Photos/Hulton Archive

First motorised fire engine 1902

London's public fire-fighting service was still in its infancy when this photo was taken in 1902. Between the Great Fire in 1666 and the late 1800s, fire-fighting in the capital was undertaken by private insurance companies. But after several large conflagrations in the 19th century, notably the 1861 Tooley Street fire, the cost of compensation became too high, and in 1866 the government formed the publicly funded and managed Metropolitan Fire Brigade. New technological developments included motorised fire engines (to replace horse-drawn ones) – the first s pictured here – a telegraph alarm system and breathing apparatus for firemen. The MFB was renamed the London Fire Brigade in 1904.

Rischgitz/Hulton Archive

Kennedy siblings
1939

Joe, Kathleen and an unrecognisably young
John F Kennedy arrive at the Houses of
Parliament two days before Britain declares
war on Germany. The trio were in town
because their father, Joseph P 'Joe' Kennedy,
was the US Ambassador to Britain at the time.
All three died tragically young: Joe, the eldest
and a US naval pilot, was killed on a flying
mission over Suffolk in 1944 (aged 29),
Kathleen died in a plane crash in France
in 1948 (aged 28) and JFK, of course, was
assassinated in Dallas (aged 46) three
years after becoming the 35th president
of the United States. Joe Senior's term as
ambassador ended abruptly following his
controversial declaration during the Battle of
Britain that 'democracy is finished in England'.
Fox Photos/Hulton Archive

Self-service job centre
1971

The country's job centres have been through many a face-lift over the years since their beginnings as Labour Exchanges in 1910. This 'groovy' incarnation from the early '70s – London's first self-service Employment Exchange – was presumably an attempt to give unemployed people a greater sense of self-determination. Job-seekers had more opportunity to choose a suitable form of employment for themselves rather than having one dished out to them, though whether or not the jaunty phrases in jazzy fonts and bright colours (orange and pink predominate) had an impact on the morale of the city's unemployed is not proved. What's certain, however, is that more people were out of work at the end of the decade than had been at the beginning.

Popperfoto

Ruth Ellis 1954

She may have been Welsh by birth, but Ruth Ellis will forever be associated with London. She lived and worked as a nightclub manager at 37 Brompton Road, Knightsbridge; she shot her lover David Blakely outside the Magdala pub in Hampstead on Easter Sunday, 10 April 1955; and she was hanged at Holloway Prison (the last woman to receive the death penalty in Britain). Her *crime passionnel* might have been forgiven in France, but Ellis's admission that she intended to kill Blakely meant a death sentence was mandatory. Despite a public outcry and newspaper campaigns for a reprieve, she was executed just three weeks after her trial, by Albert Pierrepoint. This photo was probably taken in her flat, one of a series of intimate images by a certain 'Captain Ritchie'.
Hulton Archive

Covent Garden Market 1910

The enormous piazza at Covent Garden was the site of England's largest daily fruit and vegetable market for almost 300 years, from the mid 17th century until its relocation to Nine Elms in 1974. During that time the privately owned market thrived and grew, while others, such as St James's, Newport and Lowndes Markets, were short-lived, unable to expand to accommodate the city's fast-growing populace. By the late 19th century the sprawling and hugely profitable Covent Garden site was selling everything from china and crockery to bread and liquor, but fruit, veg and flowers were its mainstay. Much of the produce was local and fresh, transported overnight from some 15,000 acres of market gardens strung around the capital, arriving at the market as early as 3am.

Hulton Archive

Terence and Shirley Conran 1955

The Conrans were already a celebrity couple when this photo was taken as part of a shoot for *Picture Post* that contrasted the evening revelries of two London couples under the heading 'Twenty Shillings or Twenty Pounds' (the article was never published). Despite the modern furniture in their apartment, it was another decade before Terence transformed the nation's homes with the launch of Habitat, but he had already opened his first London restaurants: Soup Kitchen, on Chandos Place, in 1953 and the Orrery, on the King's Road, in 1954. He met Shirley at the latter, where she was employed as a waitress. She became a professional success in her own right as a journalist and novelist, most famously for her lifestyle manual *Superwoman*, which coined the phrase 'Life is too short to stuff a mushroom'. The couple divorced in 1962.
Thurston Hopkins/Hulton Archive

Sleeping in the Underground 1940

To avoid the Luftwaffe's bombs during the Blitz, Londoners fled to tube stations, sheltering in cramped, claustrophobic and unhygienic conditions well below street level – even sleeping on the escalators when the platforms were full. The might of Nazi Germany's air force was felt by Britain, and the capital in particular, with nightly attacks that went on for three months from September to November 1940. Initially the government was unwilling to let tube stations be used (fearing they might engender a 'shelter-mentality' that would see people refusing to come back up to the surface after the attacks), but following intense public pressure and some civil disobedience, 80 stations were opened, taking up to 180,000 people on some nights.

Topical Press Agency/Hulton Archive

Dock strike 1912

The Great Dock Strike of 1889, in which London's dockers won a significant pay rise and union recognition, was followed by a decade of quiet on the capital's docks. But a wave of industrial unrest hit the nation, and the capital, prior to World War I, as dockers, transport workers, miners and others pushed for better working conditions and pay. A strike erupted in 1911 and then again in the summer of 1912 when, spurred on by radical social and political reforms, the workers once again withdrew their labour. Ten weeks later, after violent clashes with mounted Metropolitan Police, they were forced to abandon their protest. During the strike, local children such as these were dependent on food handouts from social reformers like East End suffragette Julia Scurr, who organised the feeding of 7,000 youngsters.

Topical Press Agency/Hulton Archive

Tommy Steele 1957

Teen idol Tommy Steele enjoys a night out with friends at the Bread Basket coffee house in Tottenham Court Road on 25 February 1957. Just a few months earlier, Bermondsey boy Tommy Hicks had been talent-spotted while playing his guitar in the 2i's coffee bar in Soho; the very next day he made a recording at Decca studios, and soon after was commanding £150 a night and was well on his way to a long career as a pop singer, film star, stage and musical performer and all-round family entertainer. It's not the life anyone could have imagined for the young merchant seaman who'd spent his childhood playing on bombsites and swimming in the River Thames.

Charles Hewitt/Picture Post/Hulton Archive

Cecil Beaton 1930

Cecil Beaton was no stranger to mirrors, which were a motif in his early work – and appropriate to his subject matter. Born in Hampstead in 1904, he tried working in the timber firm run by his father, but lasted only eight days: he was destined for another life. He got his break as a society photographer taking pictures of the Bright Young Things of the 1920s and '30s, the fashionable, self-obsessed set that included the likes of Evelyn Waugh, Stephen Tennant, Edith Sitwell, Diana Mitford and Beaton himself. Working for British *Vogue* and *Tatler*, he soon graduated to fashion models, British aristocracy, Hollywood stars and the royal family; his elegant and glamorous style has influenced myriad photographers, from Angus McBean to David Bailey and Mario Testino.

Hulton Archive

Flower sellers on Regent Street 1900

The London Stereoscopic Company, set up by George Swan Nottage, started life in Oxford Street in 1854 with a catalogue of exciting double-photographs that, when seen through a special viewer, created a lifelike 3D image. The result was an immediate Europe-wide craze; by 1856 more than 500,000 stereoscopes had been sold and 10,000 stereo images produced by the company. Subjects covered everything from European scenes to this image of flower sellers with their baskets of wares on Regent Street. By the 1860s, the fashion had shifted to the *carte de visite*, essentially a calling or visiting card with a photo on it. The LSC was quick to capitalise on this too, though its stereoscopic products continued to sell until 1922, when the firm ceased trading.

London Stereoscopic Company/Hulton Archive

Index